About t

In just over a year the Tyee has become British Columbia's leading independent online source of news and views about the province. With some of the top journalists in B.C. contributing, and millions of page views since its launch in November 2003, the Tyee breaks important political stories, offers diverse voices, and plays host to lively comment threads from its tens of thousands of readers.

Vancouver Magazine named the Tyee to its "alternative power list." AM 600 talk radio host Rafe Mair calls the Tyee "a key information source for our program." the *Globe and Mail* says the Tyee swims against "centralized opinion" with "some of the best investigative reporting in the province."

Go to www.thetyee.ca daily for a fresh angle on election coverage and for other original stories. There you may also subscribe for free to receive Tyee headlines once a week via email.

LIBERALIZED

The Tyee Report on British Columbia
Under Gordon Campbell's Liberals

David Beers

WITH

Russ Francis | Barbara McLintock
Will McMartin | Alisa Smith | Chris Tenove
and others

New Star Books | Vancouver

NEW STAR BOOKS LTD.

107 – 3477 Commercial Street | Vancouver, BC V5N 4E8 | CANADA
1574 Gulf Rd., #1517 | Point Roberts, WA 98281 | USA
info@NewStarBooks.com | www.NewStarBooks.com

Publication of this work is made possible by grants from the Canada
Council, the British Columbia Arts Council, and the Department of
Canadian Heritage Book Publishing Industry Development Program.

Conseil des Arts   Canada Council
du Canada   for the Arts   Canada

BRITISH
COLUMBIA
ARTS COUNCIL

Cover photo by Jim Labounty
Cover by Rayola Graphic Design
Printed and bound in Canada by Transcontinental Printing
First printing, March 2005

LIBRARY AND ARCHIVES CANADA CATALOGUING IN PUBLICATION

Liberalized: the Tyee report on British Columbia under Gordon
Campbell's Liberals / editor, David Beers

ISBN 1-55420-014-8

1. British Columbia — Politics and government — 2001– .
2. Campbell, Gordon, 1948– . 3. Liberal Party in British Columbia.
I. Beers, David. II. Title: Tyee (Vancouver, B.C.)
FC3830.2.l52 2005   971.1'05   C2005-901227-7

CONTENTS

■ LIBERALIZED ■

CHAPTER ONE

The Big Swerve

By DAVID BEERS

'HE'S JUST a man." The phrase tumbled out of the mouth of Gary Collins and lay there before the roomful of his fellow B.C. Liberal politicians. No one knew quite what to do with it, this sighing entreaty at a moment meant for triumphant fist pumping. Collins was delivering, after all, the warmup to the premier's keynote speech at the November 2004 B.C. Liberal convention, a prime opportunity to sum up the party's accomplishments and lionize its leader.

"He's just a man," Collins felt compelled to say of his friend, his mentor, his boss, the most powerful politician in British Columbia, Gordon Campbell. The phrase lay there and reporters picked it up and put it in their pockets to take home and examine later. Why would the finance minister need to tell us the premier was "just a man?" Was he speaking in code aimed at soothing malcontents in the room? Or was he trying to send a signal to a wider public unwilling to see Gordon Campbell as a protagonist in a good story, a guy to root for, a feeling soul at the center of hundreds of far-reaching policy changes enacted over the three and half years since he'd been swept into office?

The B.C. Liberals had in May of 2001 been granted the most decisive win in provincial history, 77 seats out of

79, a margin of victory that offered Gordon Campbell and his party a mandate to pass bold legislation and, if they had wanted, to change the very political culture of a bitterly polarized province.

That was a hero's story in the making if ever there was one, but here, before the gathered faithful, Gary Collins was instead taking this opportunity to bring "my friend Gord" down to life-sized dimensions. Way down. "Sometimes I want to reach out and smack him," said Collins. "And sometimes I know he wants to smack me."

"He's just a man."

What hung in the air with Collins' strange words were certain indicators that everyone knew. The fact that having taken power with an historic mandate and the clear backing of the province's corporate media, just these few years later the B.C. Liberals found themselves in a dead heat with a revived NDP led by a Métis former president of the BC School Trustees Association named Carole James. The B.C. Liberals believed they had a winning story to tell of an economy on the rebound. But the poll numbers for many, many months now had refused to signal citizens' firm embrace of the premier or his party. A month after the Whistler convention, for example, in December, Ipsos-Reid would find that more people believed Gordon Campbell would make the best premier (48 percent) compared to Carole James (35 percent). But when the same people were asked to summon personal feelings toward the two figures, far fewer disapproved of James (33 percent) than Campbell (59 percent). In the race to be liked as just a man or just a woman, James was far ahead.

What was it about Gordon Campbell that made it difficult for people to like him? The question had preoccupied his handlers long before he was ever elected premier. During his failed run against the Glen Clark-led

NDP in 1996, for example, he had tried to play the home-spun populist by wearing a red plaid shirt in commercials. He was derided for that, and returned to his familiar Howe Street suits. In 1999 readers of the *Vancouver Sun* opened their paper to see Gordon and wife Nancy with their two sons climbing Mount Kilimanjaro to help raise funds for Alzheimer's. "Mr. Campbell taught under the auspices of CUSO in Yola, Nigeria in the early 1970's," the B.C. Liberal website wants visitors to know. "While there he coached state championship teams in basketball and track-and-field and helped rebuild the school library. His personal commitment to literacy expanded while he was Mayor of Vancouver, when he spearheaded the creation of the new public library and was instrumental in bringing the Peter Gzowski golf tournament to Vancouver."

If that might seem a bit too self-satisfied to people who prefer a measure of pain and suffering in their leaders, Gordon Campbell could certainly lay claim to that as well. When he was a teenager his father, a heavy drinker, killed himself.

But when *Vancouver Sun* reporter Frances Bula was assigned before the 2001 election to profile Gordon Campbell — by then a public figure in B.C. for 18 years — she described a man difficult for most people to read. She found him "withdrawn, distant, cautious, brittle and tense when he is in the larger world facing strangers."

Only when moving among established business people, "The Circle" as Bula called it, did Campbell warmly shake hands and touch shoulders. Only within The Circle did Campbell reveal a "kind, funny ... even huggy" side. By the time Bula was assigned to take his measure, Campbell had made a journey (as detailed by Will McMartin later in this book) from a budget- and tax-

growing mayor to a provincial politician who styled himself as a true-believing tax warrior. Those who stood the
most to gain from tax cuts had become his Circle. And at
some point he and his handlers had given up on him trying to be anything other than what Bula saw: "a tall,
blandly attractive, silver-haired man, his back straight as
a book inside his well-cut business suit."

Indeed, if Campbell or anyone around him were con-
sciously constructing an image, it was that of the bot-
tom-line business guy. And if to voters that seemed drab,
it was a drabness welcome after the decade of colour provided by NDP personalities like Moe Sihota, Glen Clark
and Joy MacPhail. Their exuberant politicking was
joined in the public's mind with the crisis-a-day headlines produced by the province's notoriously aggressive
political press.

Voters were hoping Gordon Campbell would prove to
be not just a man, but something less (closed off to ego
and appetite) and something more (a wise and ethical

WEAKEST CHILD LABOUR STANDARDS IN CANADA

By ALISA SMITH

■ One moment, Luke MacIver
was doing his job, sorting card-
board at Wastech Services, a
Coquitlam recycling plant. The
next he was dead, crushed
under a pile of garbage when a
dump truck driver failed to see
the young worker. MacIver was
only 15 years old, making him
the youngest workplace fatality
in B.C. in the last two decades.

"Luke holds the record. I
don't want to see anyone even
younger get killed," says his
aunt, Deb Stead, who lives in
Jasper, Ontario. In the eight
years since the death of her
nephew, Stead has had little reason to fear. Now, however, the
B.C. Liberals have passed Bill 37,
which will effectively lower the
minimum working age from 15
to 12.

Result: B.C. will now have the
weakest child-labour standards
in Canada.

When the first draft of Bill 37
was introduced in May 2003,
Labour Minister Graham Bruce

healer of the province's bitter divisions). That is how Gordon Campbell advertised himself during the campaign. And that is what he promised on election night as 58 percent of the voters handed the man and his party their support: "It is time to restore people's trust," he declared. "It is time to restore people's confidence and you can count on these commitments being carried out."

What followed were a series of initiatives by Gordon Campbell that deepened, rather than patched, the fractures in B.C.'s political landscape. Whatever else you could say about the logic or purpose of these initiatives, there was no denying they produced clear winners and losers. A massive tax cut that favoured the most wealthy. A referendum on native treaty rights that pitted First Nations members against the non-native majority. The tearing up of union contracts for public service employees. The slashing of legal aid for the poor. Plans to purge welfare rolls. The steepest increase in college and university tuition fees in the country. The shutting down of

issued a press release explaining that the new legislation would increase flexibility in employment standards, eliminate red tape, and help kids as young as 12 enter the workforce. The permits were "a clear case of over-regulation," he said.

"There's deregulation and then there's unregulation," says Graeme Moore of Surrey, who worked for 21 years as an industrial relations officer for the Employment Standards Branch, beginning in the Social Credit era and quitting last year out of frustration with the Campbell government. "Essentially, there won't be child labour laws."

Since 1948, children 12 to 14 have needed permission from a parent, from their school, and from the Employment Standards Branch in order to work at regular jobs during the school year. Under Bill 37, all that will be needed is a parent's note to be kept on file by employers.

Bruce has said that he was not aware of any application that

various hospitals and over 100 schools across the province, some of them the hearts of rural towns.

Amidst such tumultuous change, those interested in knowing the perspectives of the losers had difficulty finding them in the province's mainstream media. The publisher of the *Vancouver Sun* and *The Province* newspapers, Dennis Skulsky, visited with Campbell shortly after he was elected. His newspapers' editorials had staunchly supported Campbell and the B.C. Liberals and continued to do so. Now as the new government began to remake B.C., it may have seemed (at least to those one out of three voters who had cast a ballot against the Liberals), that the *Sun*'s front page headlines were crafted by Gordon Campbell's own spin doctors.

Example: On January 26, 2002, when the Liberals introduced legislation to undo contracts and cut tens of thousands of public sector jobs, The *Globe and Mail* headlined its piece: "B.C. bills enrage public employees." The *Sun*'s take? "Patients and students first: Campbell."

CHILD LABOUR [Cont.]

had ever been denied. Moore estimates that he and his colleagues turned down one in five work permits for youth under 15, while a further three in five were approved only after changes to the terms of employment.

Among the rejects, Moore said, were applications to put kids to work as dirt-bike-riding scarecrows in a berry field bristling with unmarked wire at neck height, and to send a 12-year-old garbage picking alone

on the highway's edge near Surrey. Parents had pre-approved every one of these altered or denied applications, Moore notes.

Bruce has insisted that safety will not be a concern, as young workers will still be covered by the basic safety standards that apply by law to all workers in B.C.

According to the Workers Compensation Board of BC, five young workers (defined by the WCB as age 15-24) were killed

Those words reflected, almost verbatim, the headline on the Liberals' own press release. And on the day the Liberals rolled out a sweeping new labour code, the *Sun's* lead scoop was an "exclusive" interview with presidents of B.C.'s two leading unionized construction firms. They went on the record to say the NDP's labour policies sure had hurt their bottom line.

Was it inattention or bias that caused the *Sun* to run zero stories alerting readers to a major protest being organized by labour and other groups across B.C. for February 24, 2002? And then, the day after fourteen rallies did arise throughout the province, including 20,000 protesters on the lawn of the Legislature, was a mere half page, much of it a photo, on A4 the next day really all the attention the protests incited?

In the fall of 2001 *Sun* management began trimming back on reporters and editors (I was one of those shown the door). But all the belt-tightening in the newsroom didn't keep Pacific Newspaper Group publisher Skulsky

last year. Statistics also show that 50 percent of all workplace injuries occur in the first six months on the job. One young worker is injured every hour, and five are permanently disabled every week.

To date, no statistics have been kept for workplace accidents involving workers under 15 in B.C. That will change, says Karen Zukas in WCB's prevention branch. "We are tracking that in light of the new labour laws."

The most widespread abuses of young workers are likely to be less dramatic than death or disability. If children under 15 have a complaint about their employer, they will have to do as all adults have under changes put in place by the Liberals last year: fill out a complex, 19-page "Self-Help Kit" and present it to their boss. Industrial relations officers have found that many adults cannot complete the form properly, says Graeme Moore.

Under the old system, viable complaints triggered a formal

from dreaming up and investing millions in something called Believe BC, hundreds of pages of advertorial projecting a suddenly rosy future for B.C. industry. At the time, Skulsky revealed to me that he did not set out to make money with the advertising section. In fact the expectation of losing a possible $1.5 million didn't faze him. The money was well spent, he said, because Believe BC "enhances the credibility of the paper," by "adding balance" to news reporting, and "all the downtrodden stories about what's not good and what's not right in this province."

The series was done by consultants and in-house advertorial writers working from public relations material solicited from industries, whose members were then invited to advertise. More than a hundred Believe BC pages ran in the *Sun* and *Province*, with complementary spots showing on Global TV which was owned, like the two papers, by Canwest.

"Platforms for positive messaging" is how one hired

CHILD LABOUR [Cont.]

investigation, and if the boss was found at fault — if he had, for example, assigned overtime work without extra pay — he had to comply with the law and pay up. Now, the model is mediation and settlement, which means an employer could easily get off with paying only 50 percent of what is owed, says Moore. "That," he says, "is an incentive for non-compliance."

Putting children in the workforce caps off changes to the Employment Standards Act passed by the provincial Liberals, which cut overtime benefits, eliminated universal statutory holiday pay, and introduced the $6 per hour "training wage." Workers under 15 — almost certain to be entering the workforce for the first time — will mainly come under this new minimum wage, making them more appealing than adults to employers.

"Youth unemployment is already at 16 percent. It's not like businesses are clamouring

consultant proudly described the series. This, after musing aloud: "What, exactly, is a journalist?" "We're going to do more like this," said another Believe BC honcho. "Feedback from business and advertisers has been absolutely very positive." This is vitally important, explained the source, because during the fall, advertisers were quite unhappy with the newspaper for running so much negative news about terrorists, softwood tariffs, etc.

True, one big advertiser was not so impressed. Norske-Canada, B.C.'s largest pulp and paper producer, had to intervene with Skulsky to prevent their $25,000 ad, and promotional story, being printed on Russian-made newsprint. It caused the firm's spokesman to say "We struggle to understand how a Believe BC campaign could be credible."

But taken together, the B.C. Liberal messaging, the media coverage, the advertising initiatives, produced a remarkably consistent effect in those first years of Gordon Campbell's reign as premier. The idea was to create

---

for more workers," says Jim Sinclair, president of the BC Federation of Labour. "It's just a new source for the training wage."

BC Chamber of Commerce president John Winter said the Chamber was consulted on the child-labour changes as early as two years ago. "I can see no downside to it," he said.

As for the many groups that specifically represent children and youth, they have been left out of the loop entirely. Most did not hear about the proposed

changes until the first draft of Bill 37 hit the legislature in May. Even First Call — a coalition of 60 provincial groups including the BC Paediatric Society, BC Council for Families, Child and Youth Care Association of BC, BC Farm Women's Network, Save the Children Canada, Society for Children and Youth of BC, and the BC Teachers' Federation — was left scrambling to react to the proposed changes.

From reports published by the Tyee November 24 and 25, 2003.

in the public imagination, despite persistently poor economic statistics, a vision of a coming rising tide, the certainty that, as the moon shifts the oceans, Gordon Campbell's tax cuts were sure to improve the economy.

As the central character in this narrative, Gordon Campbell was required to play no role other than the human embodiment of the British Columbian economy. He was the banker to set in order the chaotic house finances (even if, as Will McMartin details in his chapter, those finances were not in any such chaos to begin with.) Gordon Campbell needn't be cuddly. He needed to be buttoned down. He needed, above all, to be sober.

A vivid expression of this ideal appeared on the newsstands in December of 2002, when *Vancouver Magazine* placed Gordon Campbell at the top of their list of 50 most powerful people. His cover photograph was black and white, lending a military crispness to his power suit, his jut-jawed profile, his upturned eyes squinting through the wire framed glasses that are standard issue to captains of industry and finance.

Not more than a month later, however, on January 10, 2003, a much different picture of Gordon Campbell appeared on the newsstands, this one of a bleary-eyed grinner holding a police booking board under his flushed face. Gordon Campbell had been arrested and jailed in Maui the night before for dangerous driving while seriously drunk. Even after his tearful apology two days later, including a vow to never drink again, public opinion and commentators were split over whether the premier should step down for what, in B.C., would be a Criminal Code offense.

Five days after Campbell's press conference mea culpa, he gave a scheduled speech on forest policy to truck loggers who stood and clapped. The next day the editorial writers of the *Vancouver Sun* sought to remind readers

What a difference a month makes. The Decenber 2002 issue of Vancouver Magazine *was just hitting recycling blueboxes on the west side of town when the infamous 'mugshot' made it onto the front page of daily newspapers in early January 2003.*

that Gordon Campbell was not just a man. Rather, he was the human embodiment of the British Columbian economy. And so talk of Campbell stepping down should stop, the editorial said. That was "yesterday's debate" and "too many of us are directing our energies toward getting even with the premier, rather than getting ahead with the business of the province."

Two years on, the B.C. Liberals with Gordon Campbell at the wheel find themselves still trying to pull out of a big swerve in public support. At the Whistler convention Gary Collins blamed the low poll numbers on a failure by the news media to report good news about the provincial economy. Foes of the B.C. Liberals had long been making the opposite claim, that their darker takes on B.C.'s economic trends couldn't find a hearing in the media. An incredulous Vaughn Palmer responded to Collins in his column for the *Vancouver Sun* the next day:

"If there is any aspect of the economic recovery that hasn't been reported in the past six months, I'm not aware of it.

"From *The Vancouver Sun*, page A1, June 1: 'Shoppers help B.C. economy grow at a sizzling pace: Consumer spending up seven per cent in March, second only to Alberta.'

"June 5: 'Optimism, 15,000 new jobs turn B.C. economy red hot: "We haven't seen business better in the province than we're seeing it right now:" Jim Pattison.'

"July 10: 'B.C. employment gains 40 per cent above national rate: Construction and tourism fuel spring job-growth numbers in the province.'

"And so on."

Nor can the big swerve of support for Campbell and his party be blamed on the lack of Believe BC-style advertising saturating the airwaves. The B.C. Liberals banned partisan government advertising four months before the May 17, 2005 polling day, but only after spending tax dollars to air a long series of ads extolling B.C.'s business climate. University of Victoria political scientist Norman Ruff called it 18 months of "propaganda."

The problem for the B.C. Liberals may be that Gordon Campbell's good news story about the economy is greeted with more skepticism than he would wish. There is a sense of collective breath holding as people wait to see if the promised boom plays out. It reflects an understanding that B.C. bobs on the capricious currents of global economic trends, the fluctuating demands in distant countries for our trees and minerals and gas and oil and high rise condos with harbour views.

For example, on the evening of December 3, 2004, a television viewer might have seen the ad in which super-capitalist Jimmy Pattison holds out his hand to the B.C. citizenry and, smiling, announces: "You're hired!" But the same viewer may have awakened the next day to find in his *Vancouver Sun* business section this headline: "Dollar has Pattison mulling U.S. move: B.C. billionaire will switch operations south if the dollar's strength cuts productivity here." Whatever else Gordon Campbell might claim about his policies' effects on the provincial economy, his party has no control over the value of the Canadian dollar.

Having no natural gift for popular charm, and having flashed to voters that indelible image of a jailed drunk, Gordon Campbell has no choice now but to forge on, stay with the script and play the role of B.C.'s walking, talking, ever improving economy.

But if most British Columbians continue to find Gordon Campbell difficult to like, a key reason will be this: Whatever economic gains there have been have yet to be felt throughout much of the province. And if there are more gains to come, not everyone has paid the same price, these last four years, in order to achieve them.

That is what the remainder of this book is largely about, an attempt to understand the ways in which Gordon Campbell's policies, so often pushed as economic necessities, have produced a fractured and divided citizenry, rather than consolidated support after the B.C. Liberals' dramatic election opportunity of 2001. As editor of the Tyee, an online news source, it has been my privilege to include in this book the insights of some of B.C.'s best journalists (who happen to be Tyee contributors). How did Gordon Campbell lose the female vote? Barbara McLintock will tell the story. Why are advocates for open government, who were once so encouraged by B.C. Liberal promises, now sorely disappointed? Russ Francis will explain. Why, despite B.C. Liberal generosity toward resource industries that operate in rural areas, is there so much anger in those parts of B.C.? Chris Tenove travelled the "hurtland" to find out. How have even the energy and fish farming booms in B.C., pushed proudly by the B.C. Liberals, managed to make allies out of environmentalists and locals fearing they are losing control of their own property and communities? Alisa Smith reports. And what about the central theme of the B.C. Liberals' reelection bid, their track record they say proves them to be highly competent fiscal managers responsible for pulling B.C. out of deep red ink? Will McMartin scrutinizes four years of government books and offers a very different analysis.

Why do Gordon Campbell's Liberals, having left the NDP for dead in the dust, now find themselves facing a neck and neck election in May of 2005? That's a big swerve, and the makings of a timely book.

CHAPTER TWO

Female Trouble

By BARBARA MCLINTOCK

IF THOUSANDS of British Columbians began to lose their confidence in Premier Campbell and his government during the course of the government's term, nowhere was that shift more marked than in the voting preferences of women voters. The first polls after Campbell was elected, when his government was still enjoying an approval rating well over the 50 percent mark, showed no marked difference between the preferences expressed by male and female voters. But as the Liberals' popularity began to fall, the drop was far more precipitous for women than for men.

By early 2004, the huge gender gap expressed consistently in all the public opinion polls taken had grown so large it was regularly regarded as noteworthy by the pollsters from the companies like Ipsos-Reid and the Mustel Group. The numbers of men supporting Campbell's Liberals was, for several months, running between 10 and 15 percentage points higher than the number of women supporters. If you looked at the approval ratings for Campbell personally, the gap was even greater. As many as two-thirds of all women polled were regularly saying they didn't like the job Campbell was doing.

In the worst poll, an Ipsos-Reid one in which 800 B.C. residents were telephoned in March 2004, only five percent of the women questioned said they "strongly approved" of Campbell's performance. In contrast, 50 percent said they "strongly disapproved" of the job he was doing. Another 21 percent said they "moderately disapproved," meaning more than seven in 10 women were unhappy with their premier. (For men, the disapproval rating was only 57 percent.)

Shortly after that poll was made public, the team planning the Liberal re-election was beginning to admit, at least internally, that the gender gap was a problem. The re-election team began to consider whether an advertising campaign, or some other sort of publicity, could convince women that the Liberals really were on their side. Civil servants in every ministry received calls from the Public Affairs Bureau or the premier's office, saying, "Tell us what you've done for women lately."

"'Tell us what we've done TO women' would be more like it," muttered more than one civil servant behind closed doors.

And therein lay the nub of the problem. Nearly every area in which the Campbell government was doing well was one which tended to appeal most to men. Nearly every area in which the administration was in trouble was one that was going to affect women the most.

In some cases, the government's cuts had hit women's services directly. The funding for all women's centres had been eliminated. Huge cuts in the legal aid budget had meant services for family law had been abandoned except for those in the most extreme circumstances. Subsidies for daycare had been reduced for thousands of women, even as new welfare rules were making it mandatory for them to return to the workforce.

Other policy changes ended up affecting women disproportionately even though there was no indication that the government's goal was actually to be harder on the female gender. Many of the wage rollbacks and privatizations in the health care sector fell into this category. The vast majority of the most extreme cuts hit the Hospital Employees Union, and 85 percent of HEU members are women. For a single mom trying to take home enough to survive, a forced 15 percent wage rollback was more than enough to turn her away from the Campbell Liberals. Even worse was the plight of those whose jobs were privatized out of existence; women who had worked in hospitals for a quarter century or more found the only hope they had for keeping a job at all was to accept a wage cut of close to 50 percent — if the new privatized owners would even agree to hire them.

But neither of these were the biggest problems when the Campbell government started looking at its relationship with female voters. That's because neither of these categories affected a large proportion of women voters. But a high proportion of the other service cuts Campbell had brought in affected tens of thousands of voters. And again, the voters affected were disproportionately women, who were affected by:

● *Cuts to health care services.* No matter how many times Campbell and Health Minister Colin Hansen tried to explain that funding for health care had actually increased, it was the women coping with illnesses and injuries in their families who knew that levels of service had unquestionably decreased. It was the women caught in the "sandwich generation" between the needs of their own children and the needs of their aging parents who knew that home nursing was much harder to come by, that home care support had been drastically reduced in most communities, and that it was practically impossible to have one's parent admitted to a chronic-care hospital unless the family was willing to pay a substantial sum or until the parent was just about at death's door. It was the women struggling to cope with children or other family members with disabilities or with mental illnesses who knew that the treatment they needed just wasn't out there. It was the women who went in to visit friends and families in hospitals and noticed that the standards of cleaning had dropped noticeably and the food was just about inedible in the first days of many of the privatization experiments.

● *Cuts to education.* Again, the Liberal government explained repeatedly that the funding for each pupil in the system was actually being maintained; the reason that school boards were facing "challenges" was simply that the number of pupils in nearly all school districts was declining, a simple function of changing demographics in B.C. Again, the explanation was completely irrelevant to thousands of B.C. mothers. What they saw was larger classes, a lack of help for their children who

SUPPORT ERODES FOR YOUNG, SINGLE MOTHERS

By JUDITH INCE

■ Agnes Tolbert arrived in Canada from a refugee camp in Liberia. "Some days, I didn't eat," she recalls. Her East Vancouver basement suite is unheated, rodents scurry around her floors and in her walls. "It's not healthy for my daughter," she says. But the landlord says if she can't stand the cold and the vermin, she can find somewhere else to live.

Linda Mix, the co-ordinator of the Tenants' Rights Action Coalition, says Tolbert's situation is fairly typical of the plight of young mothers. "We see a lot of young parents who are reluctant to make complaints, because they are afraid they'll be evicted."

Young parents like Tolbert who might be eligible for social housing have a long wait ahead of them, Mix says. The government scrapped the Homes BC program, which has "created a huge gap in the housing supply for low income families." And although the Human Rights Act

had learning disabilities or other special needs, a lack of money for proper supplies, or even up-to-date textbooks.

"It's ridiculous," one Grade Twelve student told me. "Not only are the textbooks so old that they're falling apart, but in every class, the teacher has to take time to explain the parts of the book that are wrong . . . to say 'don't learn that . . . it's all changed since that book was written.'"

● *Cuts to the Ministry for Children and Families.* If it wasn't their own children who were suffering from a lack of counseling programs for troubled teens or help for those caught up in a web of early alcohol or drug abuse, it was their friends' children — or their children's friends.

● *Cuts to educational programs in parks, plus the intro-duction of fees to park even for an hour to take the children for a walk.* And cuts to other environmental programs as well. For at least 20 years in B.C., polls have regularly noted that women are more deeply concerned about the

prohibits discriminating against a person based on family status, Mix says "we hear from tenants all over the province that they're turned away if they show up with their children."

Mary Clare Zak, the executive director of the Society for Children and Youth in B.C., says, "We're hearing about families having to sleep in cars."

Cuts target teen moms

At the same time, a legacy from the era of Bill Vander Zalm is dis-integrating, but it's a disappear-ing act that's largely gone unno-ticed. The former premier's oppo-sition to abortion and allegiance to family values led him to pro-mote programs allowing preg-nant teens and school-aged par-ents to finish their education.

But the Tyee has obtained a copy of a recent report that describes a decaying support system for teen parents at both the school and community level. Written by the B.C. Alliance Concerned with Early Pregnan-

environment and its sustainability than are men, who tend to focus, like the Liberals, on the more immediate economic benefits of resource development.

The gender divide on taxes

Campbell and his ministers would have been horrified had anyone thought that these cuts were particularly targeted at women. They weren't. They were, in the Liberal administration's mind, simply the "tough choices" that had to be made to get the government's finances under control and to reduce the burden of taxes and regulation on the business sector. But those tough choices had a disproportionate impact on women — and that was what was showing up in the polls.

By contrast, many of the changes that were viewed as more positive were of the sort that were liked best by men. It started with the 25 percent across-the-board tax cuts that Campbell announced practically the minute he took office. Polls across Canada, and indeed across North

SUPPORT ERODES [Cont.]

cy and Parenthood, the report cites provincial budget cuts, ministerial reorganization, and a failure of political nerve as the culprits in the loss of teen parent programs.

The Alliance report, completed in August, 2004, found that despite declining birth rates among teens, the needs of the moms and their babies have increased, and demands placed on support programs are growing. "This is reportedly due to two main factors," the report states,

"young parents are entering the system with a greater number of support needs than ever before, and a greater proportion of young parents are accessing the supports available."

There is no province-wide coordination of resources for teen parents. Programs rely on a hodgepodge of resources from government, charities, and community organizations, and all report highly unstable funding.

The Alliance report highlights problems for young parents

America, show that men over-all view tax cuts, especially income tax cuts, more positively than women do. Some analysts who come from a more feminist viewpoint argue that when those sorts of cuts are made, men tend just to see more money in their pockets. Women, on the other hand, recognize that big tax cuts are usually accompanied by big service cuts as well — and the women know that the extra money in their pocket won't be of over-all benefit to them, if they have to spend the savings paying for the services that their children, parents and families still need, but that are no longer easily accessible.

The tax cut wasn't the first decision that Campbell made very early in his mandate that offended many women throughout the province. Another was to refuse official opposition status to the New Democrats since they had been elected in only two seats — both those MLAs happened to be women. Legislation certainly allowed Campbell to do what he did, but it also gave

---

needing daycare. It notes changes to funding formulas and to eligibility for child care subsidies, and new deductions to childcare support money from income assistance payments. These have spelled problems for parents who need childcare in order to stay in school.

Hillel Goelman, the director of the Consortium for Health, Intervention, Learning and Development at UBC, says "the government is certainly putting less money into regulated child-

care." Before the Liberals came to power, $65 million went into childcare operating funds, an amount that has been whittled down to $48 million over the past three years. "And it's really hard to operate childcare with such meager funding," he says.

Kate Thompson, spokeswoman for the Ministry of Children and Families, denied that it has withdrawn support for childcare. Under this government, she said, "more access has been granted," and programs are

Campbell the discretion to offer the official opposition status to the NDP had he chosen to do so. Again, Campbell would deny vehemently that the gender of the two New Democrat MLAs had anything to do with his decision. It was, as he said frequently, simply a result of the democratic process. But more than one pundit wondered aloud if he would have made the same decision if the NDP caucus, no matter how small, had been headed by a powerful male leader.

Advocates for women were also disappointed with Campbell's first cabinet. They had become accustomed to an NDP cabinet where women regularly took on some of the most powerful positions going, including Finance Minister and Health Minister (both held at various times by Joy MacPhail). In Campbell's first cabinet, Christy Clark became Deputy Premier and also held the Education portfolio — but she was the only woman to be appointed to a major portfolio. Not just Finance and Health Services, but even the more traditionally "soft"

SUPPORT ERODES [Cont.]

"expanding." She pointed to a recent funding announcement of $33 million for daycare. However, a report from the Coalition of Child Care Advocates of B.C. says this money merely replaces a portion of the $42 million cut from the child care budget in 2004/05 alone.

A recent report by the Organization for Economic Co-operation and Development was "very critical of where Canada is; we're far behind other developed countries," Goelman says. In most de-veloped countries, governments cover about 85 percent of the childcare budgets, but in B.C., like the rest of Canada, that figure is 15 percent. "We have a market-driven model, which means that there's a belief that the marketplace will respond to the need," he says; only 14 percent of children in B.C. who need childcare are able to find it in a regulated setting, a number that is even smaller for infants.

From a report published by the Tyee December 21, 2004.

ministries like Children and Families, Community, Aboriginal and Women's Affairs, and Human Resources — all were headed by male members of caucus. Shirley Bond received the Advanced Education portfolio, and Sindi Hawkins the newly-created (but soon to be dissolved again) Ministry of Health Planning, but most of the other women were relegated to junior "ministers of state" positions. Women's Affairs itself was only a junior ministry of state held by Lynn Stephens under the male-dominated Community, Aboriginal and Women's Affairs ministry. In the same vein, Linda Reid got to be Minister of State for Early Childhood Development under the Child and Family Development ministry, and Katherine Whittred became Minister of State for Seniors' Affairs under the huge health services portfolio. And it wasn't because Campbell was cutting back on the size of his cabinet. The cabinet he appointed totaled 28, including the ministries of state, the largest ever in B.C. history.

As many women had expected, it wasn't long after the cabinet was sworn in that the program cuts began — and many of them had the expected disproportionate effect on women. One of the early battles occurred over legal aid, the funding for which was being drastically reduced over the next three years. The Legal Services Society found itself with no options but to virtually eliminate family law services except for cases involving family violence or other extreme circumstances. Women who found they had to go to court to get their former spouses to pay child support, for instance, were in almost all cases out of luck. Doubtless many more British Columbians of both sexes would have preferred to see the cuts come in the money spent to defend accused drug traffickers, pedophiles and other criminals — but the courts and the federal government had barred any major service reductions in those areas. So the LSS was left with family law and poverty law as the only available cutback options open to it. When the board couldn't stomach the service cuts that were required to meet the Liberals' new budget requirements, Campbell's government simply eliminated the board in the short-term and replaced it with a single administrator who agreed to make the changes.

'That's the world we live in'

Changes to the welfare system also hit hard at many women, especially those who headed up single-parent families. Previously a woman was declared "temporarily unemployable" — and hence able to collect welfare without showing proof she was also searching for a job — until her youngest child turned seven. Although some rumours floated for a while that the Liberals might reduce that age to one, the cabinet ended up compromising at the age of three.

But women with three-year-old children who needed to return to the workforce also needed to find affordable, safe, and reliable daycare — and the Liberals were also cutting back the daycare subsidies available for lower-income families. These changes essentially meant that a family now had to be making over $200 a month less than before to be eligible for any subsidy at all — and the level of subsidy had also decreased proportionately. Poverty advocates told of numerous women caught in a desperate catch-22 as the result of the changes. Their human resources ministry workers told them they must get a job — but the changes to the daycare rules meant that they would actually end up with less money from working than they received from welfare by the time they'd paid for daycare. The advocates warned that many women were ending up leaving their children in temporary, unsatisfactory, and even unsafe arrangements with friends, neighbours or relatives, because they had no choice.

Single mothers who were allowed to remain on social assistance, either because their youngest child was under three or because one of their children had special needs, didn't fare much better. The government cut the absolute amount they received each month, driving them further below the poverty line than ever. Human Resources Minister Murray Coell said the cuts were made because he wanted to ensure that every woman was better off working, even at a part-time or minimum-wage job, than she would be receiving assistance. But many women — and not just those in need of assistance — recognized that the ones who really suffered under that regime were most often the children who had no control over their own lives or their parents' activities.

It took only a few months before Lynn Stephens, the Langley MLA who held the position of Minister of State for Women's Affairs (it was no longer called Women's Equality), found herself in hot water with just about every women's group in the province. Stephens was quoted in her hometown newspaper, the *Langley Advance*, as saying that she was in charge of a "sunset" ministry that soon wouldn't be needed in B.C. — and in many ways really wasn't needed at that time.

Stephens told the *Advance* that if inequality still existed between men and women, it was only because of the choices women made, such as the choice to work part-time versus full time. "The opportunities are exactly the same," she said. "A single man and a single woman have exactly the same opportunities, with the same education." Although she agreed that some women were abused in their living situations, she said women should no longer be considered "oppressed."

When the reporter asked her if the impact of the government's cuts hadn't unfairly targeted some women, she agreed that the "rich get richer and the poor get poorer, that's the world we live in, the world we've always lived in." The remedy, she said was for the others — women presumably — to "make more money."

Predictably, the comments were greeted with howls of outrage from women's groups throughout the province. Many called for her resignation. All said loudly and publicly that it was clear that Stephens didn't understand the lamentable lack of viable choices that so many women face — a lack of choice that they argued was made worse by the cutbacks going on under the Liberals.

Shutting down the women's centres

But the furore did not deter the Liberals from their agenda of saving money by cutting programs that provided benefits to the more vulnerable in B.C. communities. Stephens announced that all government funding for

'CRUEL AND PUNITIVE' CUTS TO WELFARE

By ANDREW MACLEOD

■ In their "New Era" election platform, the B.C. Liberals gave no indication of what would come. But soon after they came to power in June 2001 they introduced welfare policies that set a new standard of harshness among Canadian provinces, according to *A Bad Time to Be Poor*, published by the B.C. office of the Canadian Centre for Policy Alternatives.

"A number of B.C.'s new welfare policies are radical and unprecedented in Canada," the report stated. Two policies in particular — an eligibility time limit and the requirement that claimants prove independence from their parents — "represent a fundamental shift in Canadian social policy — the denial of welfare when in need as a basic human right."

Most of the attention was directed at rules to limit "employable" people to two years of welfare payments out of every five. The first people

women's centres in the province would be cut as of April 1, 2004. Stephens and other MLAs made it clear that they had some real philosophical problems with the way many of the centres operated. From the government's viewpoint, they were too apt to work from a feminist model, rather than a mainstream social service one. They were too apt to engage in political action — and the government could see no good reason for funding groups whose main purpose appeared to be to overthrow them in the next election.

But in many of B.C.'s smaller communities, the women's centres were the only resource that women had to turn to when they were in trouble. These were communities too small to have their own transition house for those escaping abusive relationships, too small to have their own sexual assault centre for those whose dates had turned into nightmares, too small to have job-finding programs that catered to women only. The women's centres provided the only resource there was. When the government fund-

affected by this clause would have been cut from the welfare rules last April, but the Liberals blinked. They made anyone who was looking for work exempt from the cut-off. The change meant practically no one would be denied a cheque, since anyone on welfare who is deemed employable must commit themselves to job hunting in order to qualify for aid.

Some welfare watchers wondered if the time limits were just a cynical threat.

The time-limit issue aside, the new policies are still tough. A single "employable" person between the ages of 55 and 59 saw their cheque reduced to $510 from $557. An "employable" person between 60 and 64 years old faced a cut of nearly 20 percent, to $510 from $608. In July of 2004, the National Council of Welfare released a study branding B.C. rates "cruel and punitive." The report notes that since 1989 B.C. rates for a single employable person have fallen

ing dried up, the women's centres would, in almost every case, shut down, leaving the women in those communities with no woman-based resources at all. Their closure added to the perception that the Campbell government was lacking in understanding, not only of women's issues but also of problems that arose in rural British Columbia.

It was not only the Liberal government's policies that led to their declining approval ratings from women voters. Another major factor for many women was Campbell's arrest for drunk driving when on holiday in Maui early in the New Year of 2003. Campbell returned hastily to British Columbia, and went public with what appeared to most viewers to be a genuine "mea culpa" on television. He pleaded guilty to the charge, vowed to give up alcohol together (a promise which he appears to have kept), and gave up driving for what would be the term of a license suspension in B.C. Over-all, the incident damaged his standing in the polls far less than pundits predicted when the story first came to light. Indeed, many

'CRUEL AND PUNITIVE' [Cont.]

19.4 percent and are now 67 percent below the poverty line.

For those living in cities, the Liberals reduced shelter allowance below market prices. Earnings exemptions, which allowed people to keep the first $200 as an incentive to seek employment, were eliminated for everyone except the disabled. Single parents are now expected to work when their youngest child turns three, instead of the previous age of seven. People over 19 years old

have to prove they've been independent from their parents for two years before they qualify for assistance. Emergency hardship assistance is no longer available for people, said the human resources ministry's service plan, "in certain circumstances, such as when a person quits a job voluntarily, or for refugee claimants."

The ministry announced plans to lay off some 460 people of a total staff of 3,000, close 36 of its 198 offices across the province,

British Columbians said it had, at least, allowed them to see a more human side of the premier than previously. But once again, the poll results were not the same for both sexes. The arrest had much less of an effect on male voters than on female ones. In fact, Campbell's popularity went up among male voters, while it dropped even further with women. There's no reason this should be a surprise: consistently, for the past decade, women have been much more forceful in asserting that drunk drivers should be treated more harshly by the government.

It was just another incident to add to women's suspicions of Campbell's "law and order" agenda. When, several months later, Solicitor General Rich Coleman made his first moves to change B.C.'s provincial drunk driving laws in such a way that a high proportion of impaired drivers would escape a criminal record, opponents of the changes immediately started referring back to the Campbell arrest.

Somewhat peculiarly, rumours also continued to circu-

---

and cut its budget by 30 percent over three years.

The Liberals' cuts followed those made in the late '90s by the NDP government.

While the Liberals were gutting welfare, they made other moves that compound the difficulties for people living in poverty. Cuts to daycare subsidies make it even harder for single parents to work or go to school. Chopping all but a few job-training programs narrow the options for people who want to develop skills that will make them more employable. Reduced legal aid funding makes it hard for anyone who can't afford a lawyer to use the justice system; as a result, people needing spousal support after a separation have been unable to pursue their claims.

'To me it seems unfair'

After the cuts, Tara Mundy and her five-year-old daughter were eligible for about $860 monthly in welfare from the human

late about alleged mysteries in Campbell's private life — the sort of stories that, if true, would alienate most women voters even further. Not just New Democrats or other opponents of the Liberals, but even those who might be expected to support a private-enterprise government would swear they had it on the best authority that, in one or more ways, Campbell's private life was not what might be expected of a premier. In fact, not a tittle of evidence was ever produced to show that any of the stories had even a grain of truth to them — though some reporters, researchers and pundits put in a great deal of effort trying to track down the original source of the rumours. They never could. Campbell's private life appeared, in actual fact, to be unremarkable. Yet many women continued to cite the rumours as further evidence that the premier was not someone whom women should support.

'CRUEL AND PUNITIVE' [Cont.]

resources ministry. The rest of their income comes from a monthly child tax credit of about $200 from the federal government. They pay $640 a month to rent a two-bedroom apartment in Esquimalt — well under the average for the region — leaving just $440 for the month's utilities, food and any other expenses.

She works part-time at a daycare, but since the Liberals took away the earnings exemption that allowed people on welfare to keep the first $200 they earned without penalty, she finds herself no further ahead. Premier Gordon Campbell wants us to work, she said, but he's cut everything so that when we do work it's harder to get off welfare. "To me it seems unfair."

When the effects of the cuts were first sinking in, the Vancouver Island Public Interest Research Group (VIPIRG) issued a challenge to members of the legislative assembly to try the government's own web-based

Christy Clark packs it in

One story about Campbell's behaviour with women did have some basis in fact. That was the tale of the row between the premier and Surrey MLA Elaine Brenzinger, who quit the Liberal caucus to sit as an independent. To be frank, the Liberals didn't see Brenzinger's departure as a great loss. They became even more nonchalant about losing her when, several months later, she made strange allegations that a backbencher had been sexually harassing her — allegations which she was later forced to withdraw unconditionally. But a lot of women felt a little uncomfortable when Campbell agreed with Brenzinger that during one caucus row, he had told her to "Fuck off" — even though he said it was basically a joke. One might well argue that in the 21st century, there should be no difference between how a premier treats his male or female MLAs — but a lot of women, with management styles quite different from the standard male model,

---

income assistance estimator to see what they would receive if they had to depend on welfare. The estimator, which can be found on the ministry of human resources website, was posted by the Liberal government to pre-screen people for income assistance eligibility. None of the MLAs took up the challenge.

"The fact they didn't respond I think shows they can't look at how inadequate welfare is," said VIPIRG researcher Bruce Wallace.

Murray Coell, a social worker by training who was the Liberals' first minister of human resources, said at the time in an interview with Victoria's *Monday Magazine* that he didn't respond to the challenge because the people who issued it had "misinterpreted" income assistance. "I think the point is they don't understand income assistance is temporary," he said. "It's not a lifestyle."

Put another way, the money available under the income assis-

didn't think it was the sign of a good leader that Campbell was saying that to ANY of his caucus members, no matter what their gender.

And though Brenzinger personally hadn't been a particularly high-profile MLA, her departure appeared to signal the beginning of a significant exodus from caucus, with a high proportion of those leaving being women. Most didn't make as dramatic a departure as did Brenzinger. They just announced they weren't going to be running again, come May 2005. Katherine Whittred, who'd been removed from cabinet in early 2004, announced her retirement from politics. So did Lynn Stephens — who, in the end, chose not to go quietly into retirement.

But the biggest bombshell came when Christy Clark, the one woman who had appeared to be part of Campbell's inner circle, made it public that she wouldn't be running again either — and stepped down from cabinet, effective immediately. Clark didn't say anything against

'CRUEL AND PUNITIVE' [Cont.]

tance program isn't enough to live on because, well, nobody is supposed to live on it.

"We're attempting to help people into employment," said Coell.

Several times during that interview, Coell said there are 7,000 jobs available across the province to people on income assistance through the JobWave and Destinations programs.

However, by the ministry's own count there were some 112,000 people considered "employable" on income assistance in B.C. at that time. Add the number of people on Employment Insurance and anyone else looking for work, and competition suddenly looks pretty fierce for those 7,000 jobs.

Stan Hagen, who replaced Coell as the human resources minister, told the legislature on April 1, 2004, that nearly 90,000 British Columbians no longer depend on welfare because of the government's emphasis on

Female Trouble [35]

Campbell or the government; she insisted that her resignation was solely because she wanted to spend more time with her young son, Hamish.

But nearly everyone around the legislative buildings knew that Clark hadn't been nearly as happy in the previous few months as she had been in the first days of the Campbell government. For one thing, she'd lost the education portfolio which she had greatly enjoyed. In the cabinet shuffle, she'd been downgraded to Children and Family Development — a ministry that had become an inescapable bog of problems for numerous ministers ever since it had been founded by the NDP administration. Worse, she'd taken it over because its previous minister, Gordon Hogg, had had to quit under a cloud, relating to improper awarding of contracts. At the same time, the deputy minister had been fired.

Then the names of Clark's brother, Bruce, and her husband, Mark Marissen, had come up far too often in the wake of the Dec. 28 search warrants executed by police

employment.

So are most welfare recipients leaving for work? Some surely are, but the government's main tool for checking, the exit surveys that look at what people are doing six months after they leave welfare, raises more questions than it answers. Many people who work with the impoverished are unconvinced there's enough work available.

Under the current economic system there will never be a job for every single person who wants one, said Cindy L'Hirondelle, the coordinator of the Status of Women Action Group. Indeed, she added, our market economy needs a certain number of unemployed people to provide a willing, even desperate, pool of labour and to keep wages from spiralling upwards.

To cut the social safety net out from under people in such a system is cruel, she said. "They're sentencing people to death."

From a report published by the Tyee July 9, 2004.

on the legislative buildings. Although there was no evidence whatsoever to suggest actual wrongdoing by either man, they had clearly been involved in the federal-provincial Liberal manoeuverings that had led the RCMP to seek the unprecedented search warrants.

And finally, Clark had privately let it be known that she wasn't entirely happy about the direction in which the provincial Liberals were headed. A strong federal Liberal herself and a person with a socially small-l liberal view of the world, she was worried that those with a federal Conservative bent and a strongly socially-conservative outlook were gaining ever more sway within the party. She was distressed, for instance, to find Campbell and others strongly endorsing Mary Polak as the Liberals' candidate in the Surrey-Panorama Ridge byelection. Polak was best known in Surrey as one of the school trustees who'd fought passionately to keep books about families with same-gender parents out of primary school classrooms. Clark and others saw her nomination as a symbolic gesture of inclusion for the socially conservative.

Only a few months later, Lynn Stephens would go much more public than Clark in her criticisms of Polak when Polak announced she would like to run in a Langley riding in the next general election (after her overwhelming defeat in the byelection).

In December of 2004, just four months before the official election campaign was scheduled to begin, one of the most detailed Ipsos-Reid polls undertaken showed the Campbell government was still struggling with the gender gap issue. Not only were women much less inclined than men to support the Liberals, but they'd also made it clear why. A high proportion of those questioned agreed the economy was doing very well — but it wasn't translating into likely votes or seats for the Campbell government.

And that, pollster Kyle Braid explained, was because people weren't putting the economy as the number one issue on their list. It was running in third spot, behind health care and education. And while people believed the Liberals were likely to do better than the NDP in managing the economy, they were casting their votes in favour of the NDP when the question asked was who'd do better in managing health care and education.

Those pesky women's issues just wouldn't go away.

CHAPTER THREE

In the Hurtland

By CHRIS TENOVE

DAVE Chutter, MLA for the Yale-Lillooet riding, sat at the front of the Lillooet Recreation Centre before a seething crowd. Nearly 400 people had come to vent their confusion, frustration and anger. This was February 28, 2002, just a few weeks after the provincial government had dropped the hammer on the town. More than 50 public service jobs would be cut. The local office of the Ministry of Forests was to be closed, along with the courthouse, the Legal Aid office, an elementary school, and the Human Resources office. Rumor had it that the town hospital was about to be downsized.

People in Lillooet felt like their town was being gutted, and Chutter was the local man to blame. Constituents stepped forward and, some fighting to control their animosity, accused the Liberals of betrayal. When Lyle Knight got the chance to speak, the engineering technician asked his colleagues from the town's Ministry of Forests office to stand. "I want you to look at the faces of people whose jobs you just took away," Knight told Chutter.

Another local, Stuart Douglass, threatened Chutter with a recall campaign if the Liberals didn't ease back on the job cuts: "If we go down, you go down," he warned.

Just 10 months before, Chutter had been a cattle rancher in the Nicola Valley near Merritt. Now he sat through a two-hour reprimand in front of an entire town. Throughout the meeting he fought to keep his expression placid and attentive, but everyone could see that below the table his legs were squirming in a continual dance of agitation.

It was a remarkable turn of events. Lillooet had overwhelmingly voted Liberal in the provincial elections. Bain Gair, vice-president of the Lillooet Chamber of Commerce and publisher of the *Bridge River-Lillooet News*, says that many people blamed the New Democrats for the sluggish town economy. With the Liberal victory, he says, a glint of optimism returned to Lillooet.

"We all thought the Liberals would put the province's fiscal house in order and build a strong provincial economy, one that would benefit Lillooet as well, " says Gair, a trim man with short hair greying at the temples, dressed in our provincial uniform of jeans and a fleece jacket. "So to have them turn around and kick us in the teeth was difficult."

That sentiment has reverberated throughout the province for much of the last three years. Everyone knew that the Liberals were going to make cuts to the public sector. Gordon Campbell had won a mandate to reduce taxes by trimming waste. But when the layoffs began, it felt like a buzz saw at work rather than a surgeon's scalpel. And while the job and service cuts affected thousands of individuals in the Lower Mainland and Victoria, many rural British Columbians felt that entire communities were at risk. To fight back, towns launched hunger strikes, recall campaigns, court challenges, angry protests and back-channel pleas, sometimes threatening and sometimes begging the government to relent.

If we look at some of the flash points around the province over the last four years, it becomes clear that there is a lot more at risk than jobs and services. Smaller communities throughout British Columbia have been fighting to defend their future.

But it's not like small towns were thriving before the Liberals came to power. Canada is seeing a mass exodus from hamlets and towns to cities and suburbs. In the decade before the 2001 census, the nation gained three million urbanites; the rural population, by contrast, fell by nearly 300,000.[1] Across the prairies there are grain elevators that stand like tombstones, marking the resting places of vanished farming communities. Industrial towns have shrunk and factory towns have rusted as machines replace human hands.

We now assume that economies — and nations — are led by innovation in metropolitan "city states" rather than by tapping the wealth of the land. But this doesn't

1. The extent of our country's urbanization has been somewhat exaggerated by Statistics Canada, which defines "urban" as "areas with a population concentration of more than 1,000." Lillooet is, by this definition, urban.

NAKED DEFIANCE IN BARKERVILLE. LITERALLY.

By BILL HORNE

■ Six whiskey-swilling, cigar-smoking female poker players and their male valet adorn the cover of the 2004 Nude Cariboo History Calendar. The photo is a spoof of one taken around 1900 in Barkerville, the heart of B.C.'s 1860s gold rush. But there are differences: not only are the players women, they're playing for brownies and toonies instead of dollars and gold dust. And they're naked.

Many of the sepia-toned photos in the calendar reverse gender roles in historic settings: women wield cross cut saws and pan for gold, while men cook and do laundry. The posers, including a local mayor, town councillor and the president of the area's Chamber of Commerce, braved bugs and hypothermia to raise money for Island Mountain Arts. IMA has offered arts courses in B.C.'s north Cariboo to adults and young people, beginners and professionals, for more than 27 years.

mean that small towns should be given up for dead. The B.C. economy depends on the timber, fish stocks, minerals, oil and gas, hydropower, and other resources found outside the 604 area code. Many people appreciate the tighter bonds of community, the crisp air, the slower pace, and the beckoning vistas of ocean, forest, or mountain. Whether we want to protect the small-town lifestyle or the province's resource-based industries, it makes sense to nurture vibrant, resilient communities throughout B.C.

And it is pretty clear that, to date, this goal has not been a principal concern of the Liberal government in Victoria.

The Liberals and Lillooet

Like a lot of small towns in British Columbia, Lillooet was born of a crass but powerful motivation: the desire to get rich quick. Gold-crazed prospectors — of European and Chinese descent — swept across these dun-coloured peaks and pine-cloaked valleys in the 1850s

---

The calendar comes out of a cauldron of rage and creativity in a region hard hit by the Liberals' policies.

Tiny Wells, near Barkerville, with a population of 200, was "the little town that could", when it organized a hunger strike to save its elementary school in the summer of 2002. Fifty people took part in the strike, including the mayors of Quesnel and Wells, and BC Federation of Labour President Jim Sinclair.

The hunger strike was part of a multi-pronged campaign of letter writing, demonstrations, street theatre and music which succeeded in preventing young children from being bused more than two hours a day on a winding mountain road to a school in Quesnel. The community paid a big price for its success — locals are paying extra to keep the school open — but its unorthodox and gutsy resistance inspired activists throughout the province.

and 1860s. The town they built, near the intersection of the Fraser and Bridge rivers, was then the second largest settlement north of San Francisco and west of Chicago.

You can read that fact on a sign next to the town museum and information centre on Main Street. On the same sign you learn that Lillooet — a hamlet of about 3,000 people — is "a forest industry-based community . . . fortunate to have many other economic resources. BC Rail, BC Hydro, and the Ministries of Forests and Fisheries all have regional offices in town."

Not anymore.

In the last two years, the Ministry of Forests office was cut from 35 people to a skeleton crew of five. Their former office — which the province still rents — sits empty. And BC Rail has been swallowed by CN Rail, headquartered in Montreal. At the time this book went to print, CN was planning to eliminate most of its Lillooet workforce.

These are the kind of economic blows that can cripple a town, says Bain Gair. From the tiny brick office of the

NAKED DEFIANCE [Cont.]

Then along came a bigger challenge: the "devolution" of Barkerville Historic Town, the biggest historic site in western North America. Operated by BC Heritage, it's an award-winning, giant museum of over 100 buildings and hundreds of thousands of artifacts, which comes to life every spring and summer.

All the shopkeepers, street actors and musicians dress in period costume and speak as if it's 1870. In spite of their proper Victorian clothes, they're getting really pissed off.

The Queen is not amused

In September, 2003, the government announced it was laying off more than half of Barkerville's staff, and eliminated all the security and maintenance positions. This followed a failed attempt earlier in the year to fob off the site to the private sector. The District of Wells had considered taking it over, then backed off, after realizing it wasn't financially viable.

Bridge River-Lillooet News, he helped form the town's Community Response Committee. It was the unveiling of their report that brought Dave Chutter to the Lillooet Recreation Centre on that February day three years ago.

"There seemed to be no understanding of the real difficulty that these cuts would cause," says Gair. "We were bothered almost as much by way the cuts were done — without consultation beforehand and without an attempt to help us cope emotionally and economically afterward — as with the cuts themselves."

It is difficult to read about cutbacks in a B.C. mill town without one's eyes glazing over. These stories have the dreary familiarity of accounts of highway accidents. But when you look closely at a town, and at the impact of cuts, you get a sense of the complex and wide-ranging ways that lives are ruptured.

Gair, for instance, remembers one night in the men's locker room, when he realized that most of his hockey teammates would soon disappear from town. "It becomes

---

Although entry fees don't cover the costs of maintaining Barkerville, the site attracts so many tourists to the region that the spin-offs into provincial tax coffers far outweigh its operational costs to the government.

Ironically, the private sector is already heavily involved in the operation of Barkerville through the many contracts to run shops, B&Bs, restaurants and the theatre. There's not much left to privatize. Business people in the region are exasperated by the way the government has ignored their economic arguments. And they're furious about the plan to download responsibility for the province's history onto a tiny tax base.

A bogus brochure which appeared in the summer inviting tourists to "Visit the New Ghost Towns of British Columbia" gave Barkervillians and their supporters a big boost. This guerrilla media version of official promotional material, designed by Vancouver artist and activist

very personal when your colleagues and friends are suddenly gone," he says. "Personally, I never hope to experience it again."

Ian Routley, chief of staff at the Lillooet Hospital, says that the job cuts meant the loss of a significant part of the town's middle class. They were the type of people who volunteered, who made craft sales and road races happen. "When you lose some of the best jobs in town, it changes the place's whole socioeconomic character," Dr. Routley says. And that, in turn, makes it harder to attract new physicians — a perennial concern in rural B.C. — or the young, energetic, well-educated people needed to revitalize the community.

Cutbacks tended to have multiplier effects. The loss of over $2 million in wages in Lillooet was immediately felt by businesses up and down Main Street. House prices plummeted. There were unexpected losses: several mournful pet-owners told me that the cuts led to the departure of the town veterinarian.

NAKED DEFIANCE [Cont.]

Murray Bush, cried, "See abandoned schools, hospitals, courthouses, forestry offices, entire towns!" and urged readers to write Premier Gordon Campbell about Barkerville. "Even ghost towns are becoming ghost towns!"

Tired of being ignored, Barkerville's merchants, actors, musicians and supporters decided to go en masse to Victoria, all dressed in period finery. "Queen Victoria" invited the Premier for tea on the steps of the legisla-

ture. She had of late "not been amused" by his cuts to B.C.'s heritage.

The Premier didn't show up, but George Abbott, the Minister responsible for Heritage, invited a small group of organizers inside for a meeting. He refused to budge on his government's plans to privatize Barkerville and slash its budget.

From an article that appeared in the Tyee on December 2, 2003.

Cutbacks in welfare and disability payments sent worried people to Lillooet's government offices. They found that the Legal Aid and Human Resources staff had already been cut, and they were told to get help online or from an automated telephone service. But Dale Calder, a Legal Aid paralegal in Lillooet for 10 years, says that this recommendation was useless for many of her former clients. "A lot of people I dealt with had a grade four or five education," says Calder, now a district councillor and an angry critic of the Liberal government. "People became absolutely desperate, and they kept coming to me for help. So for the first 13 weeks after my position was cut, I kept working as the Legal Aid help, but it was EI paying me rather than Legal Aid."

To make matters worse, BC Rail's passenger service was cancelled around the same time, ending all public transport in and out of town. If you had to get to court in Kamloops and you didn't have a car, you were forced to hitchhike or — as happened in some cases — wait to be arrested for non-appearance and then make the trip in a police cruiser.

Lillooet's list of woes could go on and on. But in some cases there were compromises made with the government. The town bought the courthouse, and set up a monthly circuit court. A few jobs at the Ministry of Forests were salvaged. The Lillooet Friendship Centre managed to find funding to hire a part-time legal advocate, two years after the Legal Aid office was closed.

What really upsets Bain Gair is that there were ways to lessen the blow of the cuts, if only the government had consulted with the community beforehand. He made that argument to Dave Chutter in front of the Rec Centre crowd. "At the end of the town meeting, what we got from Chutter was, basically, 'I'll take it up with the minister,'" says Gair.

He later had a chance to explain Lillooet's predicament to Gordon Campbell himself. In his brief minutes of face-time with the premier, Gair explained that the sudden loss of 50 jobs in Lillooet was like axing 43,750 of the best-paid and best-educated people in the Lower Mainland, or 5,250 in Victoria. "What kind of a reaction do you think that would cause?" he asked the premier.

Campbell, says Gair, scratched down a note and turned to the next speaker.

The citizens of Lillooet, like a lot of people throughout the province, were caught off guard by the extent of the public sector cuts. They wondered how the cuts fit into a strategy to improve the rural economy. If Gordon Campbell had wanted to prevent confusion, he could have made a campaign speech like this:

"In the past, British Columbian governments promoted economic development through public spending. The government created rail lines to link our mines and ports to North American markets. They built roads so loggers

HOW HAIDA AND LOGGERS FOUND COMMON CAUSE

By CHRIS TENOVE AND
BROOKE McDONALD

■ In June 2002, a gathering was held at the deceptively named Small Hall, a community building in the tiny coastal village of Skidegate. The island delicacy of herring roe and sea kelp, or k'aaw, was set out along with hundreds of pounds of Chinook salmon, as at a traditional Haida potlatch. By early afternoon the cedar hall was loud with drumbeats and chatter as more than 300 guests arrived.

Potlatches and communal barbecues are not rare on the Queen Charlotte Islands, but this congregation was unique, and crafted as a message. Half of the attendees were Haida, and the other half were local loggers, many of them employees of the American multinational Weyerhaeuser. The loggers had shut down the on-island logging industry for the day, their trucks and equipment left idle in the forest.

Dale Lore, a local logger,

could get at the forests. It became understood that resource towns entered into a social contract with the government — we would provide infrastructure and help them promote their economy. We would try to shield them from the vagaries of the marketplace, using policies like 'appurtenancy' — which forced forest companies to maintain sawmill jobs where public trees are harvested.

"Under my Liberal government, those days will end. My plan is to expose all sectors of the economy to the global marketplace. Under our government you will see extensive privatization, deregulation, and corporate consolidation. There will be many layoffs. We believe that new investment and income will revitalize some communities. We admit that many communities will be put under strain, and some must be allowed to wither away. The final decision rests with the markets."

Campbell didn't really have to make that speech — people who had studied his public comments and the Liberal platform had a good idea where the government

helped organize the event as a pageant of support for the Haida's legal battle for title over Haida Gwaii. (That ruling later came down as a partial victory for the Haida — the Supreme Court reiterated that the B.C. government has to consult with the Haida before it makes decisions on land under dispute.) If successful, the Haida would gain a large measure of control over the land and coastal waters, including control of resources. For years, the logging industry had fought the attempts of Haida and environmentalists to limit the harvest of the islands' forests. This group of loggers had broken rank; they believe that they would be better off with the Haida in charge of the islands, and not the provincial government or big logging.

Lore believes that companies like Weyerhaeuser aren't interested in sustaining the forests or the local community. "They use us up, spit us out, and go to the next place without a thought,"

was headed. However, observers have been caught off-guard by two aspects of Campbell's New Era. First, the Liberals have gone back on specific promises, most notably in the case of the privatization of BC Rail. Second, the political and economic transformation has been done with little regard for the most vulnerable people in the province.

"What surprises me is how mean-spirited they've been," says Paul Bowles, a professor of economics at the University of Northern British Columbia. He points to the reduction in minimum wage (the "training wage"), the changes to welfare, the closure of women's centres and Legal Aid programs. "All these things have been hitting the people who are most insecure in the work force and in society. My view is that the costs of this strategy have been borne by those who can least bear it, and the benefits have gone to people with high incomes."

Kama Steliga, the executive director of the Lillooet Friendship Centre, has come to a similar conclusion.

HAIDA AND LOGGERS [Cont.]

he said shortly after the potlatch gathering. As far as he can tell, they do so with the blessing of the B.C. government.

While this partnership was germinating up north, aboriginals in the rest of the province felt as if their fellow British Columbians were turning against them. The Liberal government under Gordon Campbell had just launched a provincial referendum to determine the direction that negotiations with First Nations would take.

A new framework for negotiations was instituted in 1992, but has so far failed to produce a single agreement. The stalled treaty process hangs on the horizon like a thundercloud, with business leaders glancing nervously about and native bands wondering when, and how much, rain will fall.

The archipelago of Haida Gwaii, "Islands of the people," is nestled under the Alaskan panhandle and separated from the British Columbian mainland by

Over the past few years she has seen an increase in the use of Lillooet's food bank to 300 people a month, about 10 percent of the town's population. She's seen an elderly couple suddenly lose their benefits and try to survive on a combined income of less than $370 a month. She's been told that because Lillooet has fewer than 5,000 people it cannot have a problem with homelessness, making the town ineligible for related funding. "Tell that to the people living under the bridge outside town," she says.

Steliga points out that there have been some improvements under the Liberals. For instance, she applauds the premier's attention to early childhood education. Lillooet now offers a limited amount of free pre-school to anyone who wants it. "I really believe in the Liberals' motto 'Communities taking care of communities,'" she says. "But the cuts took away our ability to do that. They were too deep, too broad, too fast, and without enough forethought. There just didn't seem to be any kind of humane strategy to deal with social health."

treacherous waters and high winds.

The Haida culture — with its ornate totem poles and rich oral literature — evolved over thousands of years on the islands. It nearly became extinct at the end of the 19th century when settlers brought the smallpox virus. The epidemic cut the local population from around 9,000 down to 588 by 1911. The Haida now number about 2,000, roughly one-third of the island's inhabitants.

In February 2002, the Haida scored a legal victory against the province and Weyerhaeuser. The Haida argued that because they have a reasonable chance of proving title, they should be consulted regarding forest management on the islands. Instead, the B.C. government had gone ahead and granted Weyerhaeuser a license to log 1.2 million cubic metres of timber a year. The B.C. Court of Appeals listened to the Haida argument, and found in their favour.

Did the Liberals have a strategy for rural British Columbia? The party's New Era platform made few references to small town issues, aside from assurances that they would get the "health and education services they need." Early in the Liberal term, the most significant rural-directed policy was, arguably, the unsuccessful attempt to use a provincial referendum to buttress the government's position in treaty negotiations.

Rural issues briefly seemed to take precedence in early 2003. The Throne Speech, while making no mention of the bruising year that had passed, unveiled the Heartlands Economic Strategy. The term "heartland" — borrowed from the American political arena — was sprinkled across the province like confetti. Jim Beatty of the *Vancouver Sun* noted that on February 18, 2002, "Kamloops MLA Kevin Krueger used 'heartlands' 32 times in a single speech, proudly declaring himself from the heartlands, an advocate for the heartlands and a defender of the heartlands."

HAIDA AND LOGGERS [Cont.]

"The Crown had gone on as if there is no such thing as aboriginal title," says Guujaaw, elected president of the Haida Nation."We proved they can't do that."

In a landmark ruling on the Haida case last November, the Supreme Court of Canada stated clearly that the B.C. government must consult with aboriginal groups before they allow companies to log, mine or otherwise alter disputed land. The Supreme Court decreed that this obligation to consult is the responsibility of the province, and not of third-party groups like Weyerhaeuser.

Locals band together to preserve logging jobs

Dale Lore was elected mayor of the island community of Port Clements in late 2002, but for most of his 17 years on the Queen Charlotte Islands he's been a logger. Over that time he's converted from a self-confessed redneck to someone with a lot of

How well has the "heartland" strategy been received? Just try saying the word in B.C.'s Interior or North and see what response you get.

'You Flatbushers . . .'

"Don't you dare call us the heartland," an angry citizen of Wells told me one night in early November, 2003. It was bitterly cold outside, a record low for that time of year, and a half-dozen people had gathered in the pickled, orange light of the Legion Hall to drink Molson and play pool. But the presence of a journalist from Vancouver offered the chance for another recreational pursuit: belly-aching.

"All you down in Flatbush," the fellow growled, using a term he had coined for the Lower Mainland, "you Flatbushers just rape and pillage small communities!"

A local mining engineer joined in. "You see, when you write a column for a newspaper, it adds no value to the economy" — ouch! — "but if we go out and extract min-

respect for the land. His family has adopted local customs like filling their freezers with smoked salmon, venison and chanterelle mushrooms. "We don't have money for Kraft Dinner, but there is plenty of food to be hunted and gathered," he said.

Lore set up the Small Hall meeting as the inauguration of the Haida Gwaii/Queen Charlotte Islands Forest Workers Association, whose goal is to keep logging jobs on-island now and in the future. He claimed that the partnership with the Haida came about because the loggers — the ones who actually live on the islands — want to stick around. That means that the island resources and jobs have to be shepherded for future generations. He also suspects that the Haida will win their land claim, and that non-aboriginal residents need to prove their solidarity now. "Once the Haida have aboriginal title, and don't particularly need any co-opera-

erals or timber, that's different. We're keeping this province alive.

"But people in Flatbush," he said, savoring the new word for a moment, "reap all the benefits."

It was easy to understand their frustration. Wells was struggling. When the mayor goes on hunger strike over one provincial cutback, and concerned citizens mount a costumed protest in Victoria over another, you know it's been a bad year.

What made Wells remarkable was that people heard about the town's struggles. While Lillooet's plight went unnoticed, Wells made it into newscasts and editorials.

Why? Part of the reason is that Barkerville — the nearby historical village — is a popular tourist draw, and one of the few brand names from the B.C. Interior. But more importantly, a few people in Wells saw that times had changed, that their MLA wasn't going to stick up for them, and that their only hope was to try to jack into the Lower Mainland's news cycle.

HAIDA AND LOGGERS [Cont.]

tion with us," said Lore, "it will be difficult to say, 'Hey, help me out. I'm the guy that wasn't a good neighbour.'"

The Haida and resident non-Haida share everything from logging crews to school sports teams. They also share a growing resentment towards the provincial government and Weyerhaeuser. The stories that circulate around town often focus on island residents versus outsiders, regardless of race.

The province signed a proto-col agreement in 2001 with eight coastal First Nations — including the Haida. Called the Turning Point agreement, it committed the groups to environmentally responsible logging and land-use planning in the forests stretching from the northern tip of Vancouver Island to the border with Alaska.

Part of the muscle behind the process came from the organized environmental movement, including the David Suzuki Foundation. In 1999, the foundation

One of the people to come to this conclusion was district councillor Judy Campbell.

"We realized that we had to get into a media battle," Campbell told me when she arrived at the Legion later that evening. "Otherwise the town would slip away and disappear."

Campbell is one of those remarkable people who help hold rural communities together. She volunteers, she writes letters, she smoothes ruffled feathers in town and helps families who are struggling. In return she savours the backcountry trails, the crisp air, and the blend of fierce individualism and tight interdependence.

Thirty years before, Campbell had quit graduate studies in Calgary and took a coin out of her pocket. She needed to decide whether to go to Wells, where she had spent one summer doing an archaeological dig at Barkerville, or to Bragg Creek in Alberta. The coin landed and she pointed her car over the Rockies.

Since Campbell arrived, Wells has shrunk from more

hosted a conference for the leaders of First Nations communities along the B.C. coast, to help define the common ground that became the basis of the protocol agreement.

"Often I think environmentalists in the past used Native people," says Suzuki, describing previous partnerships to protect areas against logging or development. "We used them by saying, 'Yes, this is your land.' And then the minute they got the land [protected] the environmentalists moved on and said, 'Okay, now it's your problem.'"

"My attitude now is that if we get involved with them, it's a lifetime involvement," he says. Suzuki now believes that what environmentalists need to say is: "I am making this place my home and I have no intention of moving — and if a logging company brings in a 15-year logging plan I tell them 'Get lost. Bring back a 500-year logging plan.'"

A version of this article has appeared in This Magazine.

than 700 full-time residents to about 200. Nearby mines have shut down and funding for the local tourist draw, the Barkerville historical village, crested and fell sharply in 2003. (See "Naked defiance," p. 40.) "The last few years are the absolute lowest point I've ever seen," she said.

But the final blow for Wells, said Campbell, would be the loss of its school. "Parents don't want to put their children on a bus for two hours every day. If we lose the school, we lose our ability to attract young families to town."

'Save Our Schools'

Quite a few B.C. towns have faced the same predicament. Since the 2001 school year there have been 113 school closures, most of them rural. District school boards have shut down schools in response to declining enrolment and tight resources. Rural schools receive provincial funding on a per-student basis, and enrolment has fallen by 26,000 over the last three years. Despite these constraints, a task force commissioned by the Ministry of Education in 2002 recommended that schools are the "heart of the community" and they should only be closed as "a last recourse."

"The rural school represents more than a place for the children to be educated," the report said. "In many ways, it also represents the right to preserve a rural culture and a viable economic development plan."

Around the province, communities have made desperate attempts to save their schools. In Forest Grove, angry parents tried to occupy their school throughout the summer of 2003 after the school board ordered it closed. In Wells, citizens tossed around ideas, including a blockade of major provincial highways. But the mayor, Dave Hendrixson, had a different suggestion.

"My idea was to go on a hunger strike," Hendrixson

told me. "I didn't think it was fair for us to punish people who have to use the road, and with a hunger strike the only ones hurt would be ourselves."

If there is such a thing as a typical hunger striker, Hendrixson is not it. He's in his seventies, with short-cropped white hair and a face that's youthful but wrinkled, as if make-up had been used to age him for a movie role. He's also a guy who likes his food.

"The first week was pretty bad," he told me. "After that, you kind of get out of the habit of eating, until it starts to affect your health."

After 33 days of juice only, and 35 pounds lost, the mayor was rewarded in two ways. First, he could dine again. ("I wanted to eat a whole pizza but could only manage a single piece. It was pretty good, though.") Second, the media came. They rang his phone, they took pictures. Wells was on the map.

Of course, media attention is not a victory — it's a bargaining tool. Wells struck a deal and bought the school off the province for $1. They now pay building costs — over $10,000 a year — and the school board agreed to pay one teacher's salary. It's been a real struggle to keep the school, Judy Campbell told me, but it's worth it. "I don't want Wells to become another of one of Gordon Campbell's ghost towns."

Prince George, eventually

Prince George is in no risk of becoming a ghost town, but on November 3, 2003, it felt like the northern city was fighting for its life. That night about 800 people gathered outside city hall, stamping their feet and rubbing their hands in the stinging cold. They held a thicket of signs with phrases like "Save BC Rail" and "Gordon no more lies!" The crowd was electrified and expectant — not for the chanting and speeches but for the battle that would soon be fought inside City Hall over a city council resolution to put the brakes on BC Rail's privatization.

For much of the last century, BC Rail was the stitching that held the province together, binding communities and economies as well as hauling out timber and coal. The railway linked Prince George to fellow Northern and Interior communities, towns like Fort Nelson, Quesnel, Fort St. James, and Lillooet. It was also a link between the Interior and the Lower Mainland, a connection that many in Prince George feel is tenuous.

BC Rail had a symbolic and historical resonance in Prince George (its original name, PGE, was said to stand for Prince George, Eventually), but its citizens are practical people and most talk was about economics. A survey by the BC Federation of Labour found that 69 percent of residents believed that the Prince George economy would be hurt by schemes to privatize the railway. Not only did the railway employ 400 people in town, paying out $20 million in wages, it spent another $20 million at

HEALTH-CUT REVOLTS FLARE ACROSS PROVINCE

By JANET FRENCH

■ You may have seen them in your neighbourhood. Lawn signs reading "We're watching you" and "How many surgeries were cancelled today?" are creeping across B.C.

Signs that reflect anger over cuts to health services are just one tactic adopted by groups formed across the province in the past two years. Groups in the Interior, on Vancouver Island, and in the Lower Mainland are taking creative approaches to their advocacy because, they say, negotiating with the government and its agencies alone is a waste of time.

The Delta Health Coalition is one group whose members became tired of talking. Coalition steering committee member Al Webb says the community is still suffering from cuts the Fraser Health Authority made to the Delta Hospital two years ago. The coalition has lost patience with the boardroom,

local businesses. Four hundred local businesses and citizens took out a full-page ad in the *Prince George Citizen*, telling Campbell not to sell or privatize the railway.

The Liberals were keenly aware of the city's attachment to the Crown corporation. Shortly before the 1996 election, Gordon Campbell had announced that a Liberal government would privatize BC Rail. Many credit that statement with his party's narrow loss that year. Campbell learned his lesson. Before the 2001 election he stated emphatically that the railway would not be privatized or sold.

So, on that November night, there were howls of indignation from the crowd when Ron East, a local businessman and head of the Prince George Committee to Save BC Rail, took the stage and said: "Gordon Campbell, you lied to us!"

"You broke your word, not just to those of us who worked to get you elected," shouted East, who was co-chairman of the campaign to elect Liberal MLA Pat Bell,

says Webb. "We are of the opinion that if we can create a big enough disturbance and embarrass this government in as many ways as we can, and embarrass the Fraser Health Authority, then we can have some sort of a reprieve."

After a failed campaign to recall their MLA Val Roddick, who they say spearheaded the cuts to B.C. hospitals, the coalition appealed to the Corporation of Delta to take the Fraser Health Authority to court.

At the urging of the health coalition, Delta city council set up a phone hotline in April for patients to call with their hospital horror stories. Those stories would be used as ammunition in the court case, says Webb. "What they're doing to Delta, and what they're doing to Delta patients, is next to criminal," he says.

The lawsuit is a last resort. Community groups have met repeatedly with the health authority but without success.

"but you also broke your word with your voters, your MLAs, and many municipal councils throughout our province.

"You have no mandate, no moral right to sell off a major asset of the province without the approval of its shareholders!"

If you looked around the gathering outside City Hall, you could see the gruff union organizers running the PA system and coordinating speeches. It was the unions who had distributed information to journalists, printed placards, and paid for polls and advertisements. But anger was not confined to organized labour. The presence of people like Ron East and former Social Credit premier Bill Vander Zalm — two ardent opponents of the New Democrats and their union backers — illustrated the breadth of opposition to the BC Rail deal.

"I never thought I'd share the platform with the BC Federation of Labour," said the Zalm when he took the stage. He paused to bask in the crowd's cheers — an old pop-

HEALTH-CUT REVOLTS [Cont.]

"You've got to smack them with a two-by-four," says Webb.

Delta isn't the only B.C. community to try taking a health authority to court.

The Nelson Save Our Services group launched a suit in July 2002, saying the reorganization of health services in the West Kootenays violates the Canada Health Act and the Charter of Rights and Freedoms, which state all Canadians should have equal access to adequate health care.

Robin Cherbo, president of the Nelson SOS, says the society is collecting incident reports as evidence lives are at risk. The SOS also has more than 50 volunteers who take turns sitting in the emergency room and observing patient care. Many patients' lives are at risk, they say, because they are often transported to Kootenay Boundary Hospital in Trail, an hour's drive away, over winding mountain roads.

ulist's vice — and then continued. "It tells us that we all share the same concerns. What is at risk is not just jobs. Instead of the people of the province having some say of how we develop the economic opportunities here, it'll be someone in Montreal or in the U.S., dictating what's best not for us but for themselves. This particular asset is one of the few things left that gives us a little sovereignty."

The rally ended when a BC Rail conductor took the stage and shouted "All aboard to the council." That night Prince George's city council debated a motion, put forward by Brian Skakun, to demand that the provincial government institute a two year moratorium on BC Rail's privatization and enter into full public discussion over the railway's future. It was an impressive display of representative democracy. The councillors had clearly agonized over their decision. Before a rapt crowd, they made long speeches — not just about the future of BC Rail but also about their hopes and concerns for Prince George and the North.

Patients benefit, says government

Tara Wilson, a spokesperson for the Ministry of Health, says regionalizing health services in key centres such as Trail benefits patients, because it provides British Columbians with more specialists closer to home. Specialists are hard to recruit, and Kootenay residents used to travel much further to Kelowna or Vancouver for treatment, she says. Adding more services in Trail has reduced the number of trips across the province.

However, two recent high-profile cases have bolstered the SOS's case. Thirty-year-old Demitria Burgoon nearly died last fall after her spleen burst in a mountain biking accident. Nelson doctors saved her life, says her mother Marilyn, by breaking the rules and operating on her in town instead of sending her to Trail.

In March, Edward Morritt died after being transported to

Throughout the debate, Mayor Colin Kinsley, a stalwart supporter of the Liberals' position on BC Rail, fought to rein in the boisterous crowd. "We don't allow cheering and signs of emotion," he scolded them at one point. The crowd booed in response. Finally the motion passed, and the crowd whooped and cheered out into the cold night.

The council's resolution was, of course, completely ignored in Victoria.

Mayor Kinsley clearly anticipated that outcome when I talked to him the day after the city council vote. He had been in the Liberals' inner circle on BC Rail, in regular consultation with local MLAs and Transportation Minister Judith Reid. And he admitted that the Liberals had done a poor job of arguing their case. "The provincial government communication on this has been absolutely pathetic," he told me. "If there was ever an example of how not to communicate on a public policy, this has been it. . . . Maybe [Prince George city] council hasn't been as

HEALTH-CUT REVOLTS [Cont.]

Trail. He ruptured his spleen when he took a tumble in his Nelson garden. The SOS and Morritt's family claimed Morritt would have lived if services hadn't been cut from the Nelson hospital.

The health ministry's Wilson says politicians in Victoria won't intervene in regional decision-making. She says the government allocates funds to regional health authorities and regional district health boards, and they make the decisions about how the money is spent. It wouldn't make sense for politicians in Victoria to make local decisions when they're not sufficiently familiar with the region's needs, she says.

But other groups protesting health cuts keep popping up all over the province — including in New Westminster, Port Alberni, Kaslo, Castlegar and Revelstoke.

From a report published in the Tyee, June 21, 2004.

well informed about this as they should have been. I may be partly to blame for that."

The mayor explained that his priority had been to ensure that the integrity of the rail line was maintained and that possible benefits to Prince George were pursued. The privatization, he said, was inevitable.

That inevitability still rankled Ron East when I talked to him a year after the railway privatization, in November, 2004. "It's obvious that the decision was made before the last election," East said. "All our debating and hollering was for nothing."

Back before the 2001 election, when he was co-chair of Liberal Pat Bell's campaign, East had attended strategy meetings where Gordon Campbell was asked about his plans for BC Rail and other Crown Corporations. "He was emphatic that they were quite safe, that BC Rail would not be sold," said East. "But he was hardly elected more than a week before he started to change his tune."

If the Campbell Liberals win a second term, East fears that BC Ferries, BC Hydro, and ICBC will all be at risk of privatization. Premier Campbell, said East, "will promise he won't do it, and then do it anyway. It's that disregard for a mandate and for the democratic process that has many of us really discouraged."

The lack of a mandate to sell Crown Corporations is particularly galling, said East, because privatization is irreversible. The Liberals say that BC Rail was merely leased, not sold. But the entire BC Rail management infrastructure has already been integrated into CN, and media digging revealed that the lease can be extended a farcical 990 years. The only reason the railway was leased rather than sold, East believes, was to avoid conflict with aboriginal claims to BC Rail's right-of-way. By leasing the railway rather than selling it, the province and CN hope to leave those claims unresolved.

East's disenchantment puts him in a bind in the coming election. He worked hard to help evict the New Democrats from power, and he doesn't want to see them return. But he no longer trusts the Liberal party that he helped to elect. "We just didn't know what Campbell's real plans were," he said.

Squinting into the future

Here is one vision of rural British Columbia's future: The young, educated, and upwardly mobile continue to trickle out of the hamlets and resource towns and into the cities. The people who remain tend to be impoverished, poorly educated, and elderly — those who don't see the shining opportunities of urban life. Resource exploitation continues — perhaps it even increases — but the workforce is seasonal or housed in temporary work camps. They don't spend much money in the local communities. Most industry profits flow to the Lower Mainland or to corporate headquarters outside the province. Some small towns boom as resort destinations or retirement idylls (think of Tofino and Chemainus) but many others become increasingly poor and desperate, slowly shrinking and then disappearing.[2]

There are advantages to this situation. Public services can be delivered more efficiently in urban areas, due to economies of scale. Also, when people are packed into denser communities their per capita ecological footprint tends to be smaller — residences are generally tinier, public transit is possible, heating is more efficient. And cities these days are vibrant places of multicultural swirl,

2. Take the example of Wells. The town is desperate for new blood, new incomes, and hopes were raised when International Wayside began drilling for gold on nearby Cow Mountain. But, for the most part, the miners stay in the motel and leave their families behind.

technological innovation, and the opportunity to find your own niche to inhabit. After all, more than half of British Columbians have chosen the metropolitan life.

Why, looking at the big picture, should we worry about the loss of small town life?

"That's a question that could only be posed under the current political conditions, and I think it indicates our tremendous poverty of imagination," says Bruce Milne, a former mayor of Sechelt and professor of political science, now collaborating with the University of British Columbia on a five-year study of coastal communities.

Milne argues that our society would be impoverished by the loss of small towns and the sensibilities they cultivate. When you live in a smaller community, he says, you are forced to see yourself as dependent upon and integrated with other people. You can't become as specialized or niche-bound as cities allow. In fact, he believes that Canadians deserve the chance to choose among a diverse palette of lifestyles. "We can be more of ourselves if there are more options available," he says. "It's not just about giving small town citizens the chance to go be doctors and lawyers in the city. It's also about giving the children of those doctors and lawyers the chance to go back to the country, to cut down trees or fish or live in a quiet place and write poetry for a living."

The key is diversity, says Milne. Smaller communities provide alternatives to cities in terms of political organization, economic activity, social networks, lifestyles, values, and ways of interacting with the natural world. "A society with diversity will always be stronger than a mono-culture," he says. "It's more resilient to change."

There are also strong economic arguments for small communities, says Greg Halseth, the Canada Research Chair in Rural and Small Town Studies at the University of Northern British Columbia.

"There are lots of ways that business can be done more efficiently in small towns," he says. These go beyond having a stable workforce for resource extraction. Improvements in information technology allow companies to locate production and management components all over the world — the most obvious example being the call centres that pop up everywhere from Bombay to Scarborough to Surrey. Compared to cities, small communities offer lower tax rates, property values, and commercial rents.

To make use of these advantages, however, small towns need to attract and retain dynamic, entrepreneurial, well-educated residents. That shouldn't be impossible. When Halseth asks his students to identify the best characteristics of small towns, they list the old standbys: "safe," "friendly," "strong sense of community," "good place to raise kids or grow old," and so on. Then he tells them to look at the Real Estate section of the *Vancouver Sun* — advertisements for suburbs and housing developments use the exact same qualities to lure homebuyers.

SMALL TOWN JUSTICE

By CHRIS TENOVE

■ Early in its term, the Liberal government drastically cut funding to the Legal Services Society of British Columbia, the independent body that supplies legal aid. The LSS lost close to 40 percent of its budget between 2001 and 2004, and it was forced to slash full-time legal staff from 147 to 21 and replace 60 offices around the province with nine regional centres. Legal aid is no longer provided for poverty law (which includes issues like tenancy and income assistance) or for family law (except in cases of family violence or when children may be removed from the home.) Criminal cases still warrant legal aid, but, according to several lawyers and social advocates interviewed by the Tyee, the lack of local legal aid offices makes it more difficult to secure and consult with lawyers.

To deal with funding cuts and the loss of live bodies, the Legal Services Society has centralized

"Rural places have these desirable elements — and these are also marketable elements at the start of the 21st century," says Halseth.

But to attract and keep citizens, you need services, amenities, and infrastructure. You need fibre-optic cables and decent roads. You need programs to help the community's poor, disabled, or unfortunate. You need recreation centres, decent health care, and high-calibre, dependable schools.

"It's not like Bella Coola expects to have a heart surgery unit, or that every town should get a university," says Bruce Milne. "The problem is that services have been withdrawn very quickly, and without real consultation or accommodation of the people affected."

Service cuts did not begin with the Liberals. Provincially, services declined under both Social Credit and New Democratic governments. In fact, the cutbacks to rural services started in the early 1980s with the federal government — many will remember the great post office

and automated some of their activities. There are 1-800 numbers to call to register for legal aid, now that local offices are shut. There is LawLINE, which offers advice over the phone, and LawLINK, a website that provides information on a broad range of topics.

Unfortunately, people most in need of legal aid tend not to be equipped for self-directed research and legal action. Laurence Scott, chairman of the Legal Aid Committee of the B.C. Branch of the Canadian Bar Association, argues that Internet and phone services provided by the LSS can't fill the gaps created by government cuts. "These new initiatives are inaccessible to a large number of people who formerly accessed the system," he says. "They tend to have alcohol and substance abuse problems, they tend to be illiterate or not have English as their first language, and they're often housebound, or at least without a computer.

debates of that time. In recent years, says Greg Halseth, the Canadian government has come to realize that many of these service closures weren't economically efficient. They're now trying to find innovative, cost-effective ways to re-introduce services.

Gordon Campbell's cutbacks were not only more sudden than those that came in the past, they were magnified by other policy changes. Large tax cuts and service reductions tended to reward well-to-do urban-dwellers and punish the poor and the rural. Changes in land use policies have made it more difficult to keep some profit and capital in small communities rather than metropolitan centres.

"Concern for equity across the province has really disappeared under the Liberals," says Milne, and smaller towns have seen a precipitous drop in political clout, service levels, and economic vitality.

Even if we could afford to put a shiny new school and hospital in every hamlet — and no one suggests we can

SMALL TOWN JUSTICE [Cont.]

"All this aside, you can't just go to a website and download what you need and then go up against a lawyer with 10 years' experience," says Scott. "It's a ridiculous suggestion."

While there has been no systematic research to determine the impact of the cuts, it's not difficult to collect troubling stories. Just call up Dan Webb, a legal advocate at the North Island AIDS Society in Campbell River. He'll tell you about people with Fetal Alcohol Syndrome trying to negotiate the courts with little support, or people thrown out of apartments who don't know how to challenge their evictions.

Prince Rupert family lawyer Brenda Muliner is most bothered by cases of poor mothers, unable to get legal aid, who are overpowered by lawyers hired by wealthier fathers or grandparents. "I've seen that happen about six times — when single moms either give up custody or don't fight for access," says

— there are other issues to tackle. Smaller communities need to develop their own strategies to exploit their assets. There needs to be a demographic shift in small towns so they come closer to reflecting the overall Canadian picture, including education levels and cultural diversity. And there needs to be a rehabilitation of the image of small towns — away from their frequent depiction as narrow-minded, insular, and career cul-de-sacs.

Even with the enthusiastic support of the provincial government, the revitalization of rural B.C. is a daunting task. And small-town British Columbians recognize their precarious existence. As I travelled throughout northern B.C. and the Interior, I asked people whether they preferred to be called the "heartland", the "hinterlands," or "rural B.C." Over and over I heard the self-deprecating remark:

"Why don't you just call us 'beyond Hope'?"

But rural communities in British Columbia have not given up hope. Most people I met were resolute that they

---

Muliner.

She estimates that nearly half the people she sees as duty counsel are functionally illiterate. Many sign their names with rickety letters, like children in Grade 2. It's painfully obvious that they won't be able to untangle difficult legal and familial issues after a short chat with duty counsel. "People are going thought the cracks."

'We ran out of money'

Attorney-General Geoff Plant argues that a new legal approach is needed to deal with many family and poverty law disputes. "We have made some progress in helping people rethink the idea of legal aid," he told the Tyee in February 2004, "to move beyond traditional representation in court, to include offering information and advice, toward helping them solve their own problems."

Plant believes that a pitched court battle should be the last

would not move to the city. They would find a way to make the small-town lifestyle work. And as long as there are people like Christ'l Roshard, I believe it will happen.

Roshard and her husband live just outside Lillooet, in a small white house on a bend in the Fraser River. Their tiny acreage sports a weathered old barn, a vegetable plot, a pocket-sized vineyard, and a second small home where Roshard's elderly parents live. Like a lot of small-towners, Roshard works several jobs to make ends meet. She is the town coroner, a district councilor, and the courthouse clerk on those days the circuit court is sitting. But I've also seen her buzzing around town in her little red beater, taking a meal to a hospitalized senior, transporting an injured loon, or checking on the health of the famed Hangman's Tree (now deceased).

The texture of her life would be impossible to recreate in Vancouver — whether it is the summer evenings she spends among her grapevines, or the way she knows the family dramas of almost everyone she sees in town.

SMALL TOWN JUSTICE [Cont.]

resort for many family and poverty law disputes. The reductions in legal aid provide an impetus for reform: Now that many poor people will be unable to get a lawyer for court cases, they will have to find other solutions. (That is, providing their opponent does not hire a lawyer, take them to court, and overwhelm them.)

"But the real challenge was that we ran out of money," said Plant. "The (LSS) budget reduction was part of the overall government commitment to eliminating the deficit and balancing the budget."

Many argue that the cuts to legal aid don't save money at all. Laurence Scott believes that people who represent themselves in court slow down the whole system, since judges must take time to explain rules and court processes.

Geoff Plant made a similar argument in the provincial legislature back in 2000, when he was still in opposition. He

Roshard, like a lot of small town residents, is ready to make tough decisions and sacrifices in order to preserve this kind of lifestyle.

"We've been through a heartbreaking few years," Roshard tells me during an interview over breakfast at Reynold's Hotel. "The Liberals were calling us the 'heartland' while ripping the heart right out of us. It's like they had something rotten and wanted to try to make it pretty."

But Roshard thinks Lillooet might have turned the corner. She lists off plans for a new aboriginal cultural centre, new local tourism operators, possible tie-ins to the 2010 Olympics, and a town beautification project by a local rock garden artist. By dint of hard work and gorgeous scenery, she believes, Lillooet will fight its way back to vitality.

Bain Gair, the town publisher, is slightly more pessimistic. CN is about to decide how many positions to cut in town, and Gair thinks the loss of another two dozen

---

stated that "the system does not get off lightly when the Legal Services Society is forced to cut back on services."

Law Society censures A-G

But Plant and the Liberals have strongly defended their cutbacks. When the board of directors of the Legal Services Society tried to stand firm against the cuts, the government pressured them to resign and then restructured the board so it would be dominated by provin-

cial government appointees. When the Law Society of BC officially censured Geoff Plant, arguing that the attorney-general's cuts to legal aid threatened the administration of justice, the Liberals shrugged it off.

From a report published in the Tyee February 12, 2004.

high-paying jobs would be devastating. "We're just starting to climb out of the morass and then bang! We might get hit again," he says.

"The most important thing you need to make a thriving community, a place that people want to stay and help build, is for people to believe in themselves and their future," he says. "These cuts took that away from us, and we're still trying to get it back."

Both Roshard and Gair have soured on the provincial Liberal government, and they doubt the Liberals will sweep the Yale-Lillooet riding the way they did in 2001. (Dave Chutter announced in the summer of 2004 that he will not be a candidate in the upcoming election, citing personal reasons.) They both hope that the coming elections will give the province a chance to discuss the future of rural B.C.

That discussion will have to go beyond anger and recriminations over the service cuts of the last four years. There are important questions to ask the Liberals and their rivals. What strategies will the parties pursue to help small towns exploit their own assets — which include alternate lifestyles and community relations as well as natural resources? Will the parties commit to making decisions about service levels in a way that is both public and forward-looking, so towns can plan for the future? Will party leaders commit themselves to honoring promises made about Crown corporations? Will parties announce a cohesive approach to rural B.C. that amounts to more than a public relations campaign?

After all, Christ'l Roshard told me, "Out here in the 'heartland,' we're tired of being made to feel like the poor cousin, being ignored and cut without consideration. When it comes right down to it, Vancouver and Victoria need us more than we need them."

CHAPTER FOUR

A Government More Closed, Less Accountable

By RUSS FRANCIS

RUNNING for office, the B.C. Liberals vowed "the most open, transparent and accountable government in Canada."[1] That's what their campaign platform for the 2001 election said, and it didn't stop there: "If government followed this approach, you may not always agree with its decisions, but you would always know how those decisions were made."

To advocates of open government (including myself; I report on the Legislature for a living), these words were pure music. The Liberals even acknowledged that an open-government policy could prove at times to be a problem for the government of the day. "We know this transparency would not be without political embarrassments. But we believe government should not shirk from making tough decisions in public . . . It's time to put the public interest ahead of partisan interests."[2]

Noble sentiments indeed. So how did the Liberals do keeping their promise? Though the record is mixed, unfortunately the promise has been honored more in the

---

1. *A New Era in Public Service*, a brochure issued by the B.C. Liberals in 2000.
2. *Ibid.*

breach than the observance. To their credit, the Liberals now require lobbyists to register their spin agendas on a list that is made public. And finding out the salaries of top officials is a lot easier. But the Liberals have cut the Information and Privacy Commissioner's budget and made getting freedom of information (FOI) request results slower and more expensive. They've been caught formally tracking FOI requesters, the better to handle potential bad news. They've made something of a charade of their vaunted open cabinet meetings. And immediately upon taking power, they moved to deny opposition status to the NDP's two representatives in the Legislature, undercutting a powerful check on the sitting government.

Bright spot: The lobbyists registry

To be sure, since forming the government, the Liberals have taken several steps in the direction of openness and accountability.

Perhaps one of the most useful for government-watch-

FOI FLIP-FLOP: BEFORE AND AFTER 2001

By RUSS FRANCIS

■ Before the 2001 election, the BC Freedom of Information and Privacy Association asked then-opposition leader Gordon Campbell a series of questions concerning freedom of information. In a letter dated April 17, 2001, Campbell offered some reassuring answers and, once again, emphasized that the Liberals are "in favour of increased openness and accountability to the electorate at all levels."

For example, Campbell made a commitment about the funding for the Office of the Information and Privacy Commissioner. The office is a crucial one for FOI applicants, since it is the independent agency that deals with requests for review and complaints, as well as conducting inquiries and making orders when disputes between applicants and public bodies cannot be mediated. The office is, in effect, the policing agency for FOI.

Here's Campbell's promise:

ers is the Lobbyists Registration Act, which requires anyone lobbying the provincial government on behalf of a corporation or non-profit organization to place their names on a publicly accessible registry.[3]

In 1992, the then-government of the NDP's Mike Harcourt took a significant step in curbing the power of lobbyists by banning them from the speaker's corridor in the legislature. But for reasons unknown, the New Democrats failed to take the next step by requiring them to register — something that Ottawa had done as far back as 1988. When I asked then-attorney-general Andrew Petter about the idea in 2000, he replied: "I haven't thought about it."

Fortunately, the Liberals not only thought about it; they acted. For that, advocates of open government should be truly grateful.

3. The site, operated by the Office of the Information and Privacy Commissioner of B.C., is at http://www.ag.gov.bc.ca/lra/.

"Our commitment to open government means providing a stable funding base for the information and privacy commissioner's office to ensure that the office has the resources it needs to discharge its statutory mandate." Campbell's letter went out just one month before the election, prompting a hopeful smile from some FOI activists.

What a difference a huge majority makes

Sadly, Campbell's promises and reassurances on this front rang hollow. Perhaps the single most damaging attack mounted by the B.C. Liberals on open government was what they did to the Office of the Information and Privacy Commissioner. Rather than "providing a stable funding base" for the office, which was never extravagantly funded in the first place, the

More Light: Disclosing top public salaries

I once asked the University of Victoria for the contract of its then president, David Strong. The university declined to provide one informally, instead insisting that I file a formal request under B.C.'s Freedom of Information and Protection of Privacy Act. Despite there being precedent for the full release of senior public-sector contracts, the university provided me with only an edited copy. Three sections of Strong's contract were deleted. Naturally, I appealed the deletions, and with the help of the information commissioner's office, I was eventually given the contract in its entirety. (As it turned out, there was nothing particularly scandalous about the severed sections.) Thanks to the B.C. Liberals, that rigmarole is no longer required.

On October 21, 2002, Skills Development and Labour Minister Graham Bruce introduced Bill 66, the Public Sector Employers Amendment Act 2002. The bill moved

---

FOI FLIP-FLOP [Cont.]

Liberal government slashed its budget by 35 percent over three years. Consequently, there are now long delays in appeals, and some applicants likely simply drop unsuccessful requests rather than having to endure waiting a year or more for the appeal process.

The Liberals also failed to act on Campbell's stated interest in adding the legislative assemploy to the FOI law's coverage.

As promised, FOIs would have revealed, say, what MLAs spent on office furnishings. Way back when, Campbell had said the doomed provision was needed in order to make a top priority of ensuring "that the legislative assembly is accountable to taxpayers," enhancing "public confidence in the institution of parliament."

quickly through all three stages in the house, and was given royal assent just 10 days later. Though the measure received virtually no public attention, one section of the act constitutes an important step forward in government openness. According to section 14.8, contracts of senior public-sector employees are officially public documents. The provision applies to all public-sector staff earning over a certain amount, though the cabinet has the right to exclude particular positions. The cabinet has since fixed the threshold for disclosure at the $125,000 salary level.

What is particularly welcome about the disclosure provision is its strength: any public sector contract that includes a section guaranteeing the contract's confidentiality is "null and void." As well, the law applies retroactively: any contract that was in force when the act took effect is covered, along with newer ones.

The bill forces public-sector employers to make copies of the contracts available for public inspection during normal business hours. In addition, reports relating to the contracts and filed with the agency's chief executive officer must also be made available, providing they would be disclosed to anyone making a formal freedom of information request.

From the viewpoint of open government, 2002's Bill 66 is one of the most praiseworthy — if unheralded — of all measures implemented by the Liberal government.

Stiffing the opposition

If only the Liberal record were so consistently enlightened. Instead, within six weeks of being sworn in, the Liberal government made a move that arguably took the province back to the dark ages in accountability.

The issue was the status of the two-person opposition caucus, made up of New Democrats Jenny Kwan and Joy MacPhail. According to public statements by Premier

Gordon Campbell, the two seats were insufficient to qualify the New Democrats as the official opposition. The consequences would be far fewer resources for the opposition to research the activity of the government.

Why should the Liberals care? Because the less scrutiny there is of a governing body, the more prone it is to perform badly. But that's not the way Campbell and his associates saw it in those early days of their government. The premier had claimed publicly that B.C.'s Constitution Act specifies that two seats are insufficient to form the official opposition. In fact, it does no such thing: the legislation contains no definition of the term.

When there's a question of parliamentary law in B.C., the primary authority is the text written by the legislature's own clerk, George MacMinn, *Parliamentary Practice in British Columbia*.[4] Alternatively, the British book

4. *Parliamentary Practice in British Columbia*, 3rd Edition (1997).

TRACKING, AND STALLING, MUCKRAKERS

By ANN REES

■ The provincial Liberal government has put Freedom of Information under surveillance in order to protect its political image.

B.C.'s Freedom of Information and Privacy Act was introduced 11 years ago to allow citizens a window into government activities so that they could scrutinize its actions and hold it accountable. But confidential "Advice to Minister" notes show the FOI process in B.C. has been twisted to serve as a communications tool, which allows government to scrutinize the FOI activities of law-abiding citizens who intend to hold it accountable.

The 65 communications notes obtained under FOI show that spin doctors, using a sophisticated surveillance system, routinely track and review potentially damaging requests.

All requests from media, anyone working for the opposition, lobby groups, and others who might use records to embarrass

by Thomas Erskine May, *Treatise on the Law, Privileges, Proceedings and Usage of Parliament*[5] is used.

As it turns out, MacMinn's book is silent on the issue of the requirements for forming an official opposition. May states plainly that the official opposition "is the largest minority party which is prepared, in the event of the resignation of the government, to assume office." In fact, May couldn't have been much clearer: the two-member NDP caucus should be the official opposition. Indeed, under this definition, even one seat would have been sufficient.

But Liberal speaker Claude Richmond was having none of it. The New Democrats would be known as merely the opposition, and would not be entitled to the status of "official opposition." In a July 12, 2001, statement justifying his ruling, Richmond cited just one text: *An Ency-*

5. *Treatise on the Law, Privileges, Proceedings and Usage of Parliament*, 23rd Edition (2004).

government, are automatically flagged as "sensitive" on the government-wide database. Records deemed politically dangerous are reviewed by Liberal spin doctors prior to releasing them to the requester. Delays are inevitable — with requests flagged as "high" sensitivity taking almost twice as long to process and release. In addition, troublesome requesters are often identified by name and brought to the attention of the minister responsible, a breach of privacy protections in the Act.

And the entire exercise has the blessing of cabinet ministers, and the Office of the Premier through its Public Affairs Bureau (PAB) which designed and operates the communications FOI surveillance system. Spokespersons for the Premier did not respond to repeated requests for comment.

Meanwhile, the Office of the Privacy and Information Commissioner launched an investigation following complaints from

clopedia of Parliament. Completed more than 40 years earlier, the obscure work was written by two Rhodesians (as they were then known), Norman Wilding and Philip Laundy.

According to Wilding and Laundy, the parliamentary opposition consists of "the party in the house for the time being in the minority, organized as a unit and officially recognized, which has had experience of office and is prepared to form a government with its leader as prime minister, when the existing ministry has lost the confidence of the government." However, this definition is of "the opposition" — and not of "the official opposition," which is what is at stake here.

Wilding and Laundy's book contains no definition of the term "official opposition."

In other words, Richmond misinterpreted an obscure text in relying on it to back up his ruling that the NDP did not form the official opposition.

The cost to the NDP of Richmond's ruling is in excess

TRACKING AND STALLING [Cont.]

several requesters, including this reporter, who were identified in the confidential communications notes.

How FOIs are monitored

Here's how the FOI surveillance system works: Sensitive or politically contentious requests are weeded out through an FOI monitoring system which begins at the ministry which receives the request. Each ministry logs its FOI requests into a government-wide electronic database called the Corporate Request Tracking System (CRTS) which automatically enters the sensitive flag for targeted categories of requesters such as media.

"There are a bunch of categories and we would check a sensitivity level," said Sharon Plater, director of the Corporate Privacy and Information Access Branch (CPIAB), which operates adn maintains the CRTS database for the Ministry of Management Services.

"Our criteria are, if it is media,

of $450,000 per year, which is the additional funding the caucus would have received as the province's official opposition. With the help of a handful of talented staff members, Kwan and MacPhail have done a commendable job in holding the government to account, but even New Democrats admit they likely missed some issues as a result of losing the "official opposition" entitlement.

"The impact of what we could have had done [with the extra revenue], I don't think can be overstated," says Clay Suddaby, the executive director of the NDP caucus.[6]

The Liberals may well have been comforted by the whack Richmond landed on the New Democrats by means of his ruling, but a government without the strongest-possible opposition is at risk of becoming over-confident and apt to make mistakes.

6. Interview, December 15, 2004.

if it is a political party, lobby group or something we are aware of that is in the media — we would check it as sensitive," said Plater, who added that the practice has been in place since 1993.

Additional warning flags may also be entered in the CRTS database by the ministries which receive the requests — designating them as being of low, medium or high sensitivity for the government, according to Plater.

International FOI expert Alasdair Roberts recently reported that the CRTS database used to track FOI requests, with its sensitivity ratings puts B.C. in the "vanguard" of governments that have developed computer programs to track FOI requests.

The CRTS system cost $425,000 to develop and was installed in 2000 under the then-NDP government. It is an upgrade of the 1993 tracking and monitoring system, said Plater.

From a report published by the Tyee, April 3, 2004.

Open cabinet meetings? Not quite

Another measure that might appear at first glance to be opening up the government in fact does no such thing. When the Liberals promised to hold regular "open cabinet meetings," televised live around the province, eyebrows were raised. How on earth can the executive branch of any government properly conduct its business when its meetings are broadcast and recorded verbatim for posterity?

To many, it seemed like a silly campaign gimmick, one which would soon be forgotten after the election. This, however, was one election promise that would be fulfilled — in a fashion. While retaining the name "open cabinet meetings," the government turned the events into what amounted to televised press conferences, with all ministers ordered to attend, spouting their scripts.

Whenever, sporadically, they occurred, that is. As Tyee columnist Will McMartin reported in December, 2004, the Liberals promised one open cabinet meeting a month, but over the first 41 months, the Campbell government found time for just 30 of them. And one of the Liberals' biggest promises for open cabinet meetings fell by the wayside on major budget issues like RAV. That 2001 promise: "Ensure that major capital spending decisions and land-use decisions . . . are decided by Cabinet in public, and not behind closed doors."

Still, from the Liberals' viewpoint, the meetings hold one big advantage over press conferences: while reporters are permitted to attend, they are not allowed to ask questions. And that's how, under the guise of "open government," the Liberals created a brilliant, taxpayer-funded, regular public relations exercise.

For instance, on July 17, 2001, the night before one open cabinet meeting, the cabinet met for 90 minutes at

La Bodega restaurant on Vancouver's Howe Street. Of course, since that meeting wasn't open, we'll never know what was said or done there. To be fair, "pre-cabinet" meetings are held before ordinary "closed" cabinet meetings as well. However, according to the premier's official agenda that summer, obtained under an information-access request,[7] closed, supplementary meetings were scheduled for after every open meeting — but not after ordinary closed ones.

For instance, here's how the premier's agenda for August 15, 2001 read:

9 a.m. -11.45 a.m. [Open] Cabinet Meeting
11.45 a.m.-1 p.m. Cabinet Meeting Resumes (Chambers)

It isn't much of a stretch to imagine the Premier opening the 11.45 a.m. meeting with the following: "Good morning ministers. Now that the show's over, let's get on with the real meeting."

Smothering freedom of information

Arguably the most important measure ever undertaken in the direction of open government by any B.C. government was the 1993 proclamation, under Mike Harcourt's New Democrats, of the Freedom of Information and Protection of Privacy Act. The B.C. law is stronger than any of its Canadian counterparts, and considerably more powerful than many in other jurisdictions, covering, as it does, not only government ministries and most Crown corporations, but ultimately health authorities, universities, colleges, municipal governments and even self-governing professions such as the Law Society of B.C. In all,

---

7. Records obtained via an FOI request made for *Monday Magazine*.

more than 2000 such "public bodies" are covered. The
New Democrats campaigned for a strong FOI law during
the 1991 election, and after taking over the government
benches, carried out their promise and implemented
B.C.'s first-ever FOI law. The NDP deserve considerable
praise for opening up the workings of government and
other public bodies to members of the public who pay
for it all.

But every few years, a funny thing happens with freedom of information in British Columbia. When a political
party is in opposition, it tends to be enthusiastic in its
support of the legislation — as well as being a heavy user
of its provisions. But when that party wins an election
and forms the government, it discovers that records it
would just as soon never see the light of day are becoming public, thanks to requests made under the act.
"Hmmm . . . maybe this FOI stuff isn't such a great idea
after all," is the thinking.

Especially following the 1996 election, which returned

CYBER-SHREDDING THE EVIDENCE

By RUSS FRANCIS

■ In the fall of 2003, the
province's top bureaucrat
dropped a bombshell. The occasion was a conference marking
the tenth anniversary of B.C.'s
freedom of information law.

Jaws dropped around the
room as Ken Dobell, deputy
minister to Premier Gordon
Campbell and cabinet secretary,
told 300 delegates that he
openly flouted the rules governing the way official e-mail is
handled.

First, a little background.

Under the Freedom of Information and Protection of Privacy Act, an e-mail is formally a
record in exactly the same way
that a paper document is. And,
according to procedures established in 1995 by the Office of
the Information and Privacy
Commissioner, "consequential"
e-mail must be retained. "Consequential" e-mail makes "significant statements about the
strategy of the public body on a
controversial issue," and by

the NDP to power, the then-opposition B.C. Liberals made heavy use of the act, and before long were digging out scandals large and small by the bucketful with its help.

It was at that point that New Democrats started having second thoughts. At a 1997 legislature committee meeting, sometime cabinet minister Moe Sihota referred to an estimate that the annual cost to the government of answering FOI requests was $21 million, while just $40,000 was collected from applicants for searching and photocopying in connection with the requests. "I think it's very difficult in this day and age to justify an expenditure of that amount and that little revenue in terms of a statute," Sihota told the committee.[8] "If I had won the debate in cabinet, there would be no FOI act," Glen Clark

8. Special Committee to Review the Freedom of Information and Protection of Privacy Act, November 19, 1997.

9. Reported by an attendee who spoke on condition of anonymity.

order of the Commissioner should be handled in a way that matches what we do with paper mail.

"The more senior the person involved in e-mail communications within a public body, the greater likelihood that a single piece of electronic mail can be consequential," the Commissioner wrote.

**'I delete . . .
as fast as I can'**

Yet here's what Dobell told the delegates about how he treats e-mail: "I delete the stuff all the time as fast as I can." Not just transitory e-mail, but, apparently, all e-mail. Though Dobell claimed shortly afterwards that he knew of no attempts to subvert the information-access process in the government, his remarks suggest his practices came pretty close to doing that.

reportedly told a Vancouver meeting in 1997.[9] The following year, on July 22, 1998, Clark told the legislature:
"I hope we cut more freedom of information implementa-
tion budgets."

The Liberals, naturally, had a different view at the
time. "It's not only the letter of the law but the spirit
with which it's applied that makes the difference," then-
opposition MLA Geoff Plant said in September, 1999.[10]

Besides talking supportively about it, the Liberals were
also heavy users of the FOI law. In 2000 — the last full
year of the Liberals' opposition — political parties filed
731 FOI requests of the government.[11] Though official
records don't reveal which parties filed the requests, it's
a pretty safe bet that the vast majority of them came from
the Liberals. Yet by 2002, the first full year of the Liberal
government, the number of requests filed by parties fell
to a mere 52. It is likely that almost all of those came from
the by-then resource-starved NDP opposition.

The Liberals began voicing different sentiments about
FOI soon after the May 2001 election installed them as
the governing party. A little more than six months later,
in the elegant, wood-panelled Douglas Fir Room on the
legislature's second floor, plush leather chairs sur-
rounded a huge meeting table on expensive green carpet.
Behind a glass partition, Hansard staff recorded the conversation of members of the legislature's finance and government services committee. The guest that day, November 26, 2001, was David Loukidelis, B.C.'s second
information and privacy commissioner, and the topic
was his budget. Among the committee members was
Ralph Sultan, representing West Vancouver-Capilano.

10. Interview.
11. According to records supplied by the management services
ministry.

Sultan was once the chief economist for the Royal Bank of Canada, and is one of the savviest Liberal backbenchers.

When the $21-million estimate of the cost of FOI was raised that afternoon, it was mistakenly referred to as $20 million. Sultan was astounded. "Twenty million per year?" he asked. That's a "staggering burden upon our civil servants to respond to," Sultan told the committee.

That hardly sounds like unqualified support of FOI by the government that promised to be Canada's most open, transparent and accountable. However, Sultan did repeat a useful point previously urged by Loukidelis and other information advocates: One way of reducing the cost of FOI is to release more records routinely, without a formal request, so that the government needn't spend money answering each of the roughly 5,000 requests it receives each year.[12]

Both Liberal and NDP politicians have complained that FOI amounts to the subsidization of the news media by the government. (It costs nothing to make an FOI request, though applicants can be assessed fees for searching and photocopying.) This claim is also misguided. Typically, more than two-thirds of all FOI requests filed with government ministries come from individuals; many are adopted children trying to find their birth parents.[13] Law

12. In the period January 1 to December 4, 2001, government ministries received 4,917 FOI requests, according to records supplied by the management services ministry.

13. The figures quoted in this passage are based on the average of all FOI requests filed with the central government during the period January 1, 1998 to May 31, 2003, relying on data supplied by the management services ministry. They do not include thousands more requests filed with Crown corporations, local governments, universities, health authorities, self-governing professional organizations and other public agencies outside the central government.

firms file another 12 percent of requests, while political parties make about 5 percent. News media file a mere 4 percent of FOI requests. In other words, even if news media were forced to pay full cost-recovery fees — a highly objectionable notion — FOI would still cost the province 96 percent of what it costs now.

There's another point about the purported cost of FOI. The $21 million figure, never satisfactorily verified, includes the millions the government spends to spin-doctor some of the more embarrassing stories unearthed through FOI. It's hardly fair to blame the FOI law for those costs: the government incurred them only because it screwed up. But one should bear in mind that even at $21 million, FOI is cheap.

"FOI shouldn't be cost recovery," is the way Gerald Fahey, the president of the Vancouver-based BC Freedom of Information and Privacy Association puts it.[14] Fahey notes

14. Interview, December, 2001.

PRIVATIZING YOUR PRIVACY

By JUDITH INCE

■ Will the USA Patriot Act crack open the electronic files the provincial government keeps on us all? Joyce Murray, the minister responsible for privacy, has reassured citizens that our data is locked behind electronic firewalls that snoops south of the border will never penetrate. But B.C.'s privacy commissioner released an independent investigation of the matter in October of 2004 that expressed clear concern the legislation may not go far enough.

Congress passed the USA Patriot Act after the terrorist attacks in 2001. Its powers are sweeping, and potentially international in scope, according to Micheal Vonn, the policy director of the B.C. Civil Liberties Association. That's because the Act allows the government to seize "any tangible thing-and that includes entire databases of information — from a U.S. company."

B.C. is in the midst of a privati-

that one of the goals of FOI is to produce better decisions by officials. For instance, had more details of the infamous fast ferries project been made public earlier on, the scheme might well have been halted long before its costs reached the $454 million mark. Adds Fahey: "It's somewhat patronizing to the citizenry to think that we somehow shouldn't be allowed in on the decision-making."

Making info expensive

As regular users of the FOI law in opposition, the B.C. Liberals continually complained about being hit with large fee assessments by the NDP for the records they sought. Although there is no fee to apply for the records, public bodies are entitled to assess applicants for any costs of searches that exceed three hours, as well as for photocopying. By routinely responding to requesters with heavy fee estimates, public bodies can easily discourage citizens — and opposition parties — from making requests in the first place. While it is true that fee

zation boom. The government has outsourced many functions, but the privatization of parts of the Medical Services Plan and PharmaCare has drawn the most attention. Two multimillion-dollar American firms — EDS and Maximus — have been at the centre of the concern about privacy and the Patriot Act, simply because they will be handling massive databases of personal information, and because they are based in the U.S. Under the Patriot Act, information man-aged by a company operating in B.C. but with links to an American firm is vulnerable to seizure, Vonn said.

Act shrouded in secrecy

Murray, however, disputes the strength of the American ties. In an interview with the Tyee, she said, "With our outsourcing, we are only signing contracts with Canadian companies. I mean we're already requiring that the outsourcing company is a Canadian company." In its submission

estimates can be appealed to the office of the information and privacy commissioner, that means a lengthy delay to obtain records that could easily be stale by the time they arrive.

During the estimates debate for the premier's office, on July 22, 1998, then-Opposition leader Gordon Campbell summed up his party's position on fees for FOI requests. "There are a number of things that I think we do need to do to reinvigorate our public institutions, to re-establish trust in our institutions," Campbell told the house. "Freedom of information is really one of the easier ones. It's direct; it's simple. It says simply: Make information available when people request it, as opposed to trying to stop them and sending them large bills to get the simplest information."

If Campbell was to be believed, a Liberal government would halt the practice of demanding big money in exchange for public records. Unfortunately, while I am aware of no government policy to encourage public bod-

PRIVATIZING YOUR PRIVACY [Cont.]

to the Loukidelis review, however, Maximus describes itself as "A United States-based company whose mission is 'Helping Government Serve the People.' We have international subsidiaries," it says. "Maximus provides health benefit operations in sixteen projects in the United States, and seeks to provide such services in the Province of British Columbia."

Calibrating the degree of risk is almost impossible, however, because secrecy shrouds every as-

pect of the Patriot Act, Vonn said. "The U.S. government won't release any information about the provisions of the Patriot Act we're concerned about." Under the Patriot Act, you'll never know if information is being collected about you — or why — and it's impossible to know how often the Act has been used, and for which reasons.

Likewise, the identities of judges sitting on the secret courts convened to hear applications for information made

ies to assess fees, my own experience is that there has been a sea change since the Liberals took office.

Previously, fee estimates were rare in the extreme for the hundreds of requests I make each year. Now they are the norm. Many kinds of requests that would previously have cost nothing, these days come back with an assessment of a four-figure fee. (There appear to be no official figures for the number and amount of fee estimates.)

Shutting out the public

If the late Liberal MLA Fred Gingell is remembered for one thing by advocates of open government, it is a policy he insisted on during his illustrious years as chairman of the legislature's public accounts committee.

The committee is among the more important of all of the legislature's select standing committees. Its task is the detailed examination of public spending, taking its cues from reports by the auditor general.

Despite persistent pressure from the legislature clerks

under the Act are confidential, as is the location of the court. And companies, organizations and individuals ordered to hand over private data must keep these orders under wraps, and are forbidden to reveal them even to their lawyers.

Because the provisions of the Patriot Act remove it from the public eye, and because there is no case law concerning it, Vonn contends the government has little evidence to go on when it reassures the public that private information will stay that way. "We're all arguing in a blackout here," she said.

The privacy commissioner waded into this swamp last summer, soliciting submissions from interested parties. He was swamped with dozens of reports from across the country and around the world outlining the potential risks to public information held by American owned or operated companies.

From a report published by the Tyee October 28, 2004.

— the officers of the house who provide legal and procedural advice to the legislative assembly — Gingell steadfastly refused to end public access to the committee's meetings. The clerks urged that whenever a legislature committee dealt with its report to the house, the meeting should go in camera. The urgings were largely successful, for most committees did ban the public when discussing their reports.

But to his great credit, Gingell wouldn't budge and the meetings he chaired remained open. Sadly, with Gingell gone, secrecy has returned to meetings of the public accounts committee.

Why is the admission of the public so important to the meetings? In a word, accountability. Far too often, the exchanges between MLAs during the public sessions are vapid. It doesn't require a deeply suspicious mind to imagine that once the doors are bolted shut, our elected representatives take the gloves off and say what they really think. (While there is a version of Hansard recorded during the secret sessions, it is for the eyes of staff and committee members only, and is never publicly released.)

Here's how Liberal MLA Barry Penner, a member of the finance and government services committee, explained the committee's move into secret session in December, 2001: "If we're trying to be making recommendations as a committee to the legislature, is it not appropriate that the other MLAs be the first to hear about that before the information goes elsewhere?"[15] Added Penner: "All committees go in camera when they're drafting their reports, so I think that's nothing unusual."

Penner was wrong. Besides the Gingell-headed public

15. Select standing committee on finance and government services, December 5, 2001

accounts committee, a special committee established to review the freedom of information law, which met from 1997 to 1999, considered its final report to the legislature in public sessions. Yet as far as I am aware, no constitutional crisis arose in consequence.

Without exception, all of the legislature's select standing committees now meet in secret session while debating their final reports. Perhaps the greatest irony related to closed-door meetings concerns a second special legislature committee that reviewed the freedom of information law. During the period from March 1 to May 20, 2004, the committee met nine times. On eight of those occasions, the meetings were closed for at least part of the time. In many cases, the secret sessions occupied the bulk of the meetings.

And the reason for the secrecy? So MLAs could discuss freedom of information!

Some of the material presented in this chapter has previously appeared in various forms in Monday Magazine, The Province, *and other publications.*

CHAPTER FIVE

Fueling Frustration: Energy and the Environment

By ALISA SMITH

BEYOND Hope on the Crowsnest Highway lies Princeton, a little ranching and logging town on the banks of the Similkameen River. It is a town mostly numb to exploitation, sitting as it does on large deposits of coal and copper that once brought wealth to corporations — but the last big mine closed eight years ago, laying off 275 people and leaving no lasting trace of prosperity in the town. There is a lumber mill, but the forestry industry doesn't employ as many people as it once did, there being less and less forest every year, but more and more machines. Locals believe one of the best ways to make money in Princeton is to become one of the town's slumlords.

Princeton is only the latest and best example of what has become a pattern in the B.C. government's handling of natural resources and the environment. In Princeton it's fossil fuels, but elsewhere in the province the conflict is over forestry, mining, resort development or fisheries. The pattern is still the same. A lack of consultation that riles locals. Cutbacks to environmental regulations, assessments and monitoring. Conflict with communities. And above all else, an unwavering commitment to the same 1950s-style dependence on primary resources that has fueled rural British Columbia's boom-and-bust cycle since the Social Credit days of W.A.C. Bennett.

Rancher Brad Hope stands on a bunchgrass hill over-looking his 500 acres, and beyond to the rolling grass-lands and lodgepole pines of the entire Similkameen valley. His brown and white Herefords chew the good wild grass that has been nourishing cattle since the 1860s, when American merchants fattened up their ani-mals here before continuing to the Barkerville gold fields. There is a sort of timelessness to the scene, a pas-toral contentment. But everything changed last summer.

"That's when the landmen came," Hope says. They told him that a corporation named Petrobank owned the coal-bed methane under his ranch, and they were going to do some seismic testing, the prelude to drilling. "That was news to me!" says Hope. "I've got a certificate going back to 1903 that says I own my coal rights." Hope has silver hair and sparkling blue eyes and a passion for playing and coaching hockey. He is a tall, bulky man — but he manages to look slumped and small now. That's because he's remembering the call he made to the Ministry of Energy and Mines. "They jumped all over me. They wanted to make sure we understood we had no rights. They even sent up a PR person with maps covered in arrows, circles and dots to explain it."

Hope discovered that, in 2002, the B.C. Liberals began auctioning coalbed methane rights — which had never existed before — to the highest bidder. Hope never heard about it, nor did any of the 600 or so individual coal-rights owners throughout the province. However, the largest coal companies — including top-10 Liberal party donors Elk Valley Coal and Weldwood of Canada, and regular contributors Quinsam Coal and Tembec Industries — were informed, and successfully bid on the newly created methane tenures. In 2003, the government passed the Coalbed Gas Act, which retroactively made what they did legal, and protects the government from lawsuits. The Coalbed Gas Act is a peculiar document. In it, the Liberals proclaimed that methane "must be considered to and always have been a natural gas," and that "natural gas is and always has been a mineral." They had to play God and redefine nature because these terms have an established legal definition and therefore come under government control.

In the old days, coalbed methane was the gas that killed canaries in the mines, and it had to be vented so that it didn't kill miners too. This dangerous by-product had no known use, and so was never defined by laws dealing with other resources. Coal, on the other hand, was the main fuel in colonial times, and the rights to it were often awarded to the owner of the surface plot of land. It was only in later decades that the concept of selling the underground mineral rights of private property to a third party developed.

While coalbed methane can be mixed with and burns like natural gas, it has very different properties under-

FORGING AHEAD ON FISH FARMS

By ALISA SMITH

■ While the B.C. Liberals weren't the first to allow fish farms in the province, they have certainly been the most enthusiastic advocates. In 2002, they lifted a moratorium put in place by the NDP seven years previously. This despite warnings from Norway, where scientists say the fish-farm industry has devastated wild stocks with diseases and fouled the marine environment; and the reports of B.C. scientists that yes, some of those aggressive Atlantic salmon have escaped and are displacing our Pacific salmon, and that wild pinks in the Broughton Archipelago, which has the highest concentration of farms, had an outbreak of sea lice and a 99-percent crash in their numbers. It is a peculiar attitude: what nature produces for free, scrap that, let's buy net pens and feedstock and pay employees to handle these Atlantic intruders to put on the dinner plate year round. Never mind that chefs consider

ground. Coalbed methane is contained within solid coal, gas and oil are in porous layers underground. Therefore, the latter is much easier to extract and doesn't require as many wells per square kilometre. Because coalbed methane requires low-pressure conditions to be removed, any underground aquifer over the coal must be pumped out first, and it can take months or years before the methane comes up in sufficient amounts. It's expensive to wait this long, and often the amount of gas to be had is an unknown quantity, making it less attractive to investors.

There are also environmental complications not encountered with regular oil and gas. When the deep aquifers are drained, the whole water table can fall, meaning that people's wells go dry. This deep-ground water, which usually has high salt levels, has to be disposed of somewhere. While technically it is not toxic, large amounts of it kill plant and animal life.

There is a logistical problem: Where to put a lake's worth of water? If it is injected back into the earth, it can

it an inferior product, one with grey flesh that has to be dyed the healthy blush pink of wild salmon.

The B.C. Liberals seem to share the attitude of Mark Ayranto, the development manager of Pan Fish, who wrote a letter to the *Prince Rupert Daily News* saying that critics should be satisfied because the environmental assessment for the fish-farm site at Anger Anchorage — given final approval by the federal Department of Fisheries and Oceans in July 2004, and the first of 18 hoped-for locations south of Prince Rupert — was "500 pages in length and nearly three inches thick," as though size was an automatic indicator of content.

Anger Anchorage is an apt summary for local feeling. "Fish farms as proposed are harmful to steelhead and the other wild stocks that we depend on," says Sharon Robertson, president of the North Coast Steelhead Alliance in Hazelton, a town on

spread unpredictably through fissures, again ruining local wells that supply both drinking and irrigation water. Often, the water can't be injected. In the States, that has meant draining it directly into rivers and lakes, with disastrous effects. While this is being called "the non-preferred option" in B.C., there are presently no laws against it.

"See that field?" Hope says, sitting at the kitchen table of his house, and he gestures out the large picture window. "There's an underground lake there, and that's how I irrigate the alfalfa that I feed my cattle in the winter. If that water gets spoiled, I don't have a ranch." The grassland ecosystem around Princeton is not only rare, it's delicate and extremely arid. When we were up in the hills he showed me a dip in the ground that used to be a pond that they skated on in winter, and his cattle drank from in summer. It had never been dry in living memory, but there's been a drought the last few years, and it's as though the pond never was. One farmer near the river

FISH FARMS [Cont.]

the Skeena River. "The sport fishery is the major tourism industry in the fall for all the upcountry communities. But the government did not invite us to consult, and we were not made aware of any public hearings," she says. "Though there was obviously consultation with the industry sector."

The concern follows the flow of the Skeena River to its outlet at the Pacific Ocean in Prince Rupert. "The proposed sites are in the southern approaches to

the Skeena," says Luanne Roth, president of the Prince Rupert Environmental Society. "Our economy and way of life are very dependent on the wild salmon." Her group organized a poll of residents in the spring, and found that, of people with an opinion, 71 percent were against the proposed fish farms.

Roth says that the present mayor, Herb Pond, campaigned as a fish-farm opponent, and his victory was due, at least in part, to this stance. However, he and

had to dig a new well last year, 25 feet deeper than usual, to tap into the lowering water table. On the upland benches some residents have to dig down 400 feet. This makes people in the Similkameen region particularly attentive to what happens underground.

"The government targeted Princeton, they thought it would be easy," says Hope, sipping a coffee. "It's just the way they did it, changing the law, and not telling anybody what was happening. It left a bad taste in everyone's mouth."

An auction without bidders

Across the province, the Liberals have been hustling in corporations to exploit local resources while doing their best to keep public input to a minimum. If local opinion rejects their plans, the government usually ignores it.

Word of the new methane tenures sent ripples of fear through a number of old coal-mining towns. In September 2003, the Union of BC Municipalities passed a resolu-

the city council have since passed a resolution in support of fish farms. (Pond did not return calls.) Roth says that the council has agreed to reconsider the resolution, based on an information package her group submitted to them. Local Tsimshiam band councils have come out against it, with the exception of the Kitkatla, a small band on Dolphin Island that has signed an economic agreement with Pan Fish.

Of Pan Pacific's 18 proposed sites, two (at Petrel Point and Strouts Point) are presently in the final federal review process, though there is no known completion date yet. After closing the fall 2004 legislature session after only 10 days to "save money," as they explained it, the B.C. Liberals have shifted their decision making into the closed arena of party meetings. At their November 2004 convention in Whistler, party members patted themselves on the back for cutting down fish-farm regulations, resolved to fast-track approvals,

tion (based on one made by Comox-Strathcona a few months before) asserting that whereas "local communities, including their local governments, First Nations, and potentially affected landowners have not been adequately consulted or informed," all coalbed methane activities should be suspended until "their concerns are fully considered, and until adequate policies, regulations and guidelines are enacted to ensure [their] safe development." The cool, bureaucratic language of the resolution only thinly masks outrage at everything the provincial government has done.

In early 2004 in the southern Rocky Mountains, when rights to Crown land near Fernie and the Flathead River were up for grabs, the Fernie city council passed a similar resolution. Even the Republican governor of Montana, Judy Martz, publicly expressed her concerns, because the river in the Elk Valley flows directly into their Glacier National Park. She formally requested that Ottawa ensure an environmental review would be done first. "If

FISH FARMS [Cont.]

and blasted the federal government for its red tape.

The DFO has, apparently, felt the sting of these rebukes. "We are trying to standardize the process so that it will only take six months to get site approval," says Thomson.

'Lack of clear vision'

Meanwhile, an important set of studies from the federal and provincial auditors released at the end of October critique government management of both wild stocks and fish farms. "The findings of the audit concern me," B.C. Auditor General Wayne Strelioff said in a news release for his report, *Salmon Forever*. "British Columbia's ability to ensure sustainability of wild salmon is handicapped by the lack of a clear vision to guide priority setting." And because of provincial budget cuts, he noted, "provincial efforts to manage wild salmon in their freshwater environments have diminished in recent years . . .

they want to pursue a full-scale operation that could devastate one of our most pristine and valuable areas for recreation and wildlife, then they're asking for a fight," Montana senator Max Baucus told the *Calgary Herald*. Despite all this, the B.C. Liberals went ahead with the auction in August — after all, a potential $800 million in royalties was at stake. But public opposition was so fierce, not a single company put in a bid.

Even industry shook its head at the Liberals' strategy. "The concept of fast-tracking a project like this makes no sense," Michael Gatens, CEO of the Calgary-based coalbed methane producer MGV Energy and chair of the Canadian Society for Unconventional Gas, told the *Financial Post*. "These kinds of projects, in environmentally sensitive areas, are going to take a lot of time to even make the decision to develop."

But ride your steamroller long enough and you're bound to flatten somebody. Mining company Redfern's proposed Tulsequah Chief mine for zinc, copper, silver

Existing provincial legislation and regulations do not provide adequate protection for salmon habitat, because some key provisions are either not in force or not being acted on." Notably, the *Vancouver Sun*'s coverage omitted these condemnations of B.C. government policy.

The federal auditor general pointed out that the DFO has never reported on the status of fish habitat in Canada, and that there are "significant gaps in the status of scientific knowledge about the potential effects of salmon aquaculture." Despite these obvious problems — or, more to the point, because of ignoring them — B.C. has barrelled ahead to become the fourth largest producer of farmed salmon in the world after Norway, Chile and the United Kingdom.

Prince Rupert councilor Nelson Kinney says that violates common sense: "For me, the word 'farming' should be done on land."

and gold near Atlin, in northwestern B.C., shows that the Liberals equally favour all old-school resources. Ever since the NDP gave the project the initial go-ahead in 1997, the local Taku River Tlingit have been worried — and organized.

There are bountiful salmon spawning grounds and nurseries throughout this watershed, which includes parts of B.C., the Yukon and Alaska. It is important habitat for grizzlies and mountain goat, as well as being the home range of an at-risk herd of woodland caribou, and was slated to be recognized as such by the federal government in 2005. The Tlingit still maintain a traditional routine of hunting and fishing, so the region is both a natural and cultural resource.

However, Redfern's proposed 160-kilometre road would disrupt this wild region, one of the province's last Serengetis. While Tlingit efforts through the B.C. Supreme Court won them the right to a detailed environmental assessment, the Liberal government fought the obligation to consult all the way to the Supreme Court of Canada. In fact, while the case was still in court, the provincial government gave its final approval to the project, despite all the potential environmental harm its own report showed. In November of 2004, the Supreme Court of Canada ruled favourably for Redfern, which is now waiting for a federal rubber stamp.

"The Liberals came into power with a wheelbarrow full of mining money and they were intent to hand over the Tulsequah Chief on a platter," says David MacKinnon, executive director of the Transboundary Watershed Alliance in Whitehorse. "They are more interested in cooperating with industry than safeguarding the public interest."

MacKinnon is not comforted by provincial government assurances that the road will be removed in nine years.

"History is a better barometer than the promises of a transient government. An industrial road of this size has never been deactivated in North America," he says. Past environmental damage in the watershed has yet to be addressed. There are still acid mine drainages and heavy metals leaching directly into the Tulsequah River from a short-lived 1950s mine on the same site. In 2002, the provincial government gave Redfern until 2003 to clean it up — and when the company failed to do that, the period of grace was extended to 2005. "They have an ever-expanding window of non-compliance," says MacKinnon. Critics see this as the template of the future: when government rules are loose, corporations will run through the gaps.

'I'm green at this activism stuff'

In the case of Princeton, the Liberals are counting on a time-honored strategy: dangle a wad of cash in front of a last-chance community, and you'll get some takers. The family at the old Wright ranch, near Highway 3 just west of Princeton, negotiated a lease with Petrobank to allow them to drill a test well on their property for an undisclosed sum of money. (Those who don't want to negotiate get taken to arbitration, and the government will set a rate for the intrusion.) The Wright property was in a key area of Petrobank's 37,000-acre tenure.

"Oh, everybody says Pat Wright would be turning over in his grave if he knew what his relatives did," says Madelon Schouten, a rural Similkameen resident and president of the Vermilion Field Naturalists. She has convinced this group to lobby the Liberals for an environmental assessment, and she is now setting her sights on getting the BC Federation of Field Naturalists to do the same.

"I'm very green at this activism stuff," she says apologetically. Schouten is a small plump woman wearing a white sweatshirt covered in bright bird images, and the entryway to her small house a half-hour north of Princeton is filled with cages of live birds, and glass terrariums of stuffed specimens. She has a lunch of soup and crustless sandwiches laid out on the kitchen table, just so. "But it was so peculiar when in fall 2003 all these Petrobank trucks and their red and blue flags appeared. I said, 'What are those about?' No one else knew either, but we all wondered." The more she learned about coalbed methane, the more worried she became. She puts on her glasses as we look at the large piles of documents she has assembled. "The grasslands are so fragile," she says, shaking her head.

While she says she is unhappy about how elected officials keep her at arm's length, persistence has at least gotten her into one of the government's selective meetings. "In July, we [Vermilion Forks Field Naturalists] were invited to a meeting we thought would be public. But

SOUR GAS, BOILING ANGER

By SHEFA SIEGEL

■ On the Peace River steppes of northeastern British Columbia, places with frontier names like Tumbler Ridge, Dawson Creek and Fort St. John are enjoying a boom. The fuel is natural gas, and plenty of it.

But with the boom comes high risks to workers even as the government is cutting back on health and safety officers in the region. And anger is rising among residents who hate living close to wells they say are making them ill.

Since NAFTA, Canada has quietly become the largest exporter of oil and gas to the United States. Canadian exports now account for roughly 15 percent of natural gas and 9 percent of crude oil flowing into the U.S., and these figures are continuing to climb. The action is especially hot in the Peace River region, where more than 100 oil and gas companies are competing for profit.

In Tumbler Ridge, as in many

there were only three members of what you would call the public, including myself, who were there. I didn't get anything out of it except to be puzzled," Schouten says. (Rolf Schmitt, the Ministry of Energy official in charge of Princeton's coalbed methane development, did not return calls requesting an interview.) "They told us Princeton was a test site. It's being pushed through in such a hurry. I said how can the government oversee what's going on, when they have cut back their staffing? This government says that the companies will appoint their own watchdog. But how can we trust them to do this?"

Right now, the company lets the public tour its test well on Wright Road. This has done much to convince the fence sitters that coalbed methane drilling is harmless. Opponents, though, are quick to point out that this is only one well: not the hundreds that full-scale production could involve, not the new roads that go with them. Also, because the company is only taking a sample of the

places, municipal officials have auctioned every available lot for the garages and equipment dealers needed to service industry. Property values have already more than doubled. Once production begins at least 1000 workers will be needed to operate the wells, drive the trucks, service the lines, haul water . . . and flare the stacks.

Call it the new gold rush. But if gold causes fever, natural gas makes an odour. At least half of the gas reserves here are sour.

Sour gas is rich in sulphur and surfaces in a toxic compound with hydrogen, one that emits the unmistakable scent of foul eggs.

'Knockdown' power

Standard practice in the industry is to "dispose" of hydrogen sulphide by burning it on site rather than paying to pipe it to a refinery, have it separated, and find a market for it. (Flared hydrogen sulphide also becomes toxic sulphur dioxide, or SO_2.)

earth's core less than three millimetres wide, there is no need yet to build infrastructure to hook into the gas pipelines, nor to dispose of the potentially vast quantities of displaced water.

When I visited on a rainy afternoon, the contracting company, Akita Drilling of Calgary, had reached 1.5 kilometres into the earth, and they would keep drilling until they hit either coal seams or volcanic rock. It's a fairly simple setup: a few trailers, some generators, a sorting tray of mud you can walk around in a minute, and a metal rig a few stories high with the drill attached. Where it enters the earth it is shrouded in a canvas-draped enclosure, hot from the friction of the drill even on this winter day.

The ground around the rig is scraped bare of all vegetation in a wide area, leaving only deep mud. The men on the rig look between 20 and 30, their working lives a function of metal and steam. They are economic refugees from Manitoba, Saskatchewan, all over: young hopeful

SOUR GAS [Cont.]

When inhaled in doses of more than 100 parts per million, hydrogen sulphide attacks the respiratory system, killing you in a matter of seconds. If you are lucky, the concentration is only half that, and causes what oil and gas workers call a "knockdown," where unprotected well operators stumble into leaks and instantly collapse from the toxicity.

At least two workers have died in the B.C. Peace region from sour gas in the last two years,

and the Workers Compensation Board estimates there are four or five "known" knockdowns per year.

The real number of sour gas knockdowns may be higher because a heavy code of silence is respected within the industry, say activists. But even the official figures on knockdowns and deaths are "outrageous," says Mae Burrows, Director of the Labour-Environmental Alliance. "I don't know any other industry where that level of insult to

men who converged on Calgary to get hired and sent wherever they were needed. The rig, when you are on it, could be anywhere, British Columbia or its counterpart on the other side of the world, Colombia (where Petrobank also operates). It is utterly divorced from the natural world.

'New Era' looks like the old

In their New Era platform for the 2001 election, the Liberals promised to eliminate corporate subsidies. They have erased the New Era document from their website, and a number of their promises went along with it. In fact, the oil and gas industry has more subsidies now: $103 million towards road building, and royalty reductions for drilling in summer and for marginal or deep wells. Every coalbed methane well gets a $50,000 royalty credit, and total government royalties for this resource have been cut from 27 to 13 percent. Take away these props, and the industry wouldn't go far.

workers is tolerated so openly." In fact, sour gas is deemed the most common cause of sudden death in the workplace by the National Institute for Occupational Safety and Health.

Routine, lower-level exposure to sour gas can cause neurological damage (memory loss, headaches, dizziness), reproductive disorder (miscarriages, birth defects) and, depending on who you ask, cancer. The full extent of the danger posed by sour gas, especially its carcinogenicity,

remains fuzzy to the scientific community — not because the science is in conflict but because it simply is not there. According to the Agency for Toxic Substances and Disease Registry, "Hydrogen Sulfide has not been classified for its ability to cause or not cause cancer." Similarly, the U.S. Environmental Protection Agency concludes that data is inadequate for an assessment of the carcinogenic potential of hydrogen sulphide.

"We take the threat of sour gas

What about giving some support to green entrepreneurs and power producers? This industry, supercharged by Kyoto Protocol mandates, will take off in the future. However, British Columbia looks set to fall behind in this new economy. While the Liberal decision to make BC Hydro, a government-controlled corporation, purchase power from private producers opened the door a crack to those in the forefront of wind, solar and other renewable power sources, they haven't put out the welcome mat.

"If you're writing about what the Liberals have done for sustainable energy, that must be a real short article," says Kevin Pegg, owner of Energy Alternatives in Victoria. "When they started their term, I was hopeful at first, since they are a pro-business government. But there is no support at all," he says.

There is a growing grassroots interest in solar and other energies that only needs a nudge to take off. "Our business is booming," he says. "It's mostly recreational properties where they can't hook into the grid. Everything

SOUR GAS [Cont.]

very seriously," says Jan Rowley, Shell Canada's Manager of Public Affairs. "There is no doubt hydrogen sulphide is a deadly poison. But when it gets to low concentrations there are questions. So far there has not been anything that confirms the concerns of residents, and there are lots of studies which demonstrate that workers' exposure over 50 years failed to result in ill-health effects."

Boom outrunning watchdogs

Despite the public health and labour concerns, the B.C. government's economic plan is moving full steam ahead. Canadian resource extraction is governed by 19th-century mining laws that refuse landowners rights to anything below the top six inches of the earth's surface. In short, the provincial government, not local residents, is the primary beneficiary of billions of dollars in royalties from deeply buried

from little cabins to 7,000-square-foot homes where money is no object. Name a place in B.C. and we've been there.

"Right now, there is a global shortage in photovoltaic panels because of the great new laws Germany has passed. Our suppliers are scrambling," he says. "There is a potential to make B.C. a world leader in this field. Right now, we are a world loser." Most galling, he says, is the government's reaction to Vestas, a Danish wind turbine company.

Vestas is presently scouting locations for a new factory in Canada and they have narrowed it down to three provinces, with Squamish being the B.C. choice. More than 400 jobs are involved. The company asked the B.C. government to guarantee a purchase of 1000 megawatts of wind power over five years. (To put this in perspective, BC Hydro is aggressively expanding its power purchasing by 2,000,000 megawatt-hours in the next two years.) "I'm not interested in telling BC Hydro what to

natural gas deposits.

Revenues from oil and gas have eclipsed those from timber in B.C., after the number of wells in the province grew 39 percent in a decade, creating a five-billion dollar industry the Liberal Party says it wants quadrupled by 2008.

Oversight for workers' safety and the environment hasn't kept pace. The ranks of enforcement officers working for the Ministry of Water, Air and Land Protection have been cut by 40 per-

cent under the current government. The number of Workers Compensation Board officers for the Peace River region is down from nine to six, and of those six three have been on stress leave. Another agency with major oversight responsibilities is the Oil and Gas Commission, an arm of the Ministry of Energy and Mines. Its budget remained flat this year despite the steep increase in drilling activity.

"Industry just does whatever it wants," says Stacey Lajeunesse,

do," energy minister Richard Neufeld proclaimed. Yet Neufeld didn't have any qualms about telling BC Hydro what to do when it fit Liberal ideals, such as breaking down state monopolies; in 2002, he ordered the utility to buy all its new power from private producers.

It is unclear yet whether this doctrinaire attitude will nix the deal for Squamish, though it certainly can't help. Mayor Ian Sutherland says they are still talking with the company. If Vestas sets up shop, he continues, they would become the town's biggest industry by a long shot — and they are likely to expand, making them a good long-term employer. (The largest employer right now is the wood fibre mill, and forestry in general is on the downswing.) Despite this potential, Sutherland supports the minister's decision. "Vestas can put in a bid with everyone else, and if at the end of the day their proposal is the best, BC Hydro will choose them."

However, BC Hydro appears most comfortable with regressive choices. They recently agreed to buy polluting

SOUR GAS [Cont.]

who is board director for the Peace Country Environmental Protection Association, a citizens' group founded in 1994. "There's nobody out in the backcountry to watchdog this stuff."

From ExxonMobil to Talisman, Shell and EnCana, the Peace now hosts the giants of oil and gas. With 10,000 gas wells already on-line, production is advancing north along the Alaska Highway to Fort Nelson and southwest toward Alberta, where wells share canola and barley fields with farmers who have little control over where and when new wells are drilled.

Wells a whiff away

It used to be that wells were sunk in the bush, away from populated areas. But the convenience of drilling next to people's homes — where access to roads, power and water reduces start-up costs — has companies sinking wells so close to residences that the noise of compressors and smell of flared gas are now

natural gas-fired energy from a plant to be built on Duke
Point on Vancouver Island, to the tune of 250 megawatts
a year, which is equivalent to the amount Vestas asked
for. As far as wind power goes, BC Hydro has been
finicky. While they agreed to purchase from a 58.5-
megawatt project by Wynn Stothert on northern Vancouver Island, they turned down energy from a proposed
450-megawatt wind farm by Sea Breeze, also on Vancouver Island. "What happens on a day the wind does not
blow?" BC Hydro spokeswoman Elisha Moreno told
Business in Vancouver. "Natural gas has more capacity,
and it has an ability to generate when we need it most."
Sea Breeze president Paul Manson responded that wind
energy can be stored in hydroelectric dams, like they do
in Denmark.

"You could burn tires and garbage and they'd buy it if
that was cheapest," says Guy Dauncey, president of BC
Sustainable Energy Association in Victoria. "I'm very
unhappy with the Liberals. They think fossil fuels are

part of ordinary life.

"The way the law is currently structured in British Columbia sour gas wells can be drilled within 100 metres of private homes," says Karen Campbell, staff lawyer for West Coast Environmental Law. "This is a real concern for residents, who have very little opportunity to participate in decisions about drilling on or next to their homes. Even the Oil and Gas Commission's own Advisory Committee has expressed concern about the lack of legal requirements with respect to the placement of sour gas wells."

The industry and B.C.'s government say new technologies make nearby wells safe for residents. Critics say people remain at risk of both long-term low-level and catastrophic exposure from leaks, explosions and routine flaring.

On a recent fact-finding trip paid for by environmental groups, I spent a week in the Peace region. Families there

wonderful, basically. They don't have a single plan to address global warming." Recently, Premier Campbell tried to convince Prime Minister Paul Martin to back away from Canada's commitment to the Kyoto protocol, which scientists say is still too weak to stop global warming. "We tabled a report to the [energy] ministry, stating 10 cost-neutral policies about sustainable energy that they could adopt right now, and they haven't done a thing," says Dauncey. "Yet, they are doing everything they can to support coalbed methane."

'We're walking a tightrope'

The Liberals are excited about coalbed methane because of the dollar signs. In 2003 they got $50 million from auctioning rights, and no doubt got more in 2004. The Princeton region alone could bring them $800 million in drilling royalties — part of the Liberal plan to double provincial oil and gas revenues by 2011. The government policy of secrecy makes it easier to divide and conquer

SOUR GAS [Cont.]

described the terror of feeling their houses shaken by an explosion at the nearby well, grabbing their children from bed, and dashing to their trucks as the stink of sulphur enveloped them. Women spoke of the fear of carrying infants to term with a sour well operating within spitting distance of their homes, and the constant concern over what the poisons are doing to their children.

"I don't know what it's going to take for people to wake up to what's happening here," a local told me. "We're even scared to grow a garden because we don't want to eat food from our land. We don't have any idea what's in the soil."

One couple sought me out to discuss burns on their bodies suffered after what they believed was an unpublicized leak at a nearby well. I met a number of other families who claimed their lives are in ruin because of sour wells perched within view of their kitchen

communities, and it's hard to say if the people of Princeton will fend off such a motivated assault.

"We started by protesting this [drilling], because of aboriginal rights and title we have. The province was giving away a resource that was ours. They did not consult with us. We had lawyers involved," says Philippe Batini, manager of the Upper Similkameen Indian Band, which now supports coalbed methane development. He is a small man with dark brown skin and sharp handsome features, grey cowboy boots and a thick Québecois accent. He says he is concerned with both reserve land and all their traditional territory in the Similkameen region. Since the initial standoff, Petrobank — which is based in Calgary and "didn't have a grasp of native rights here" — has become more savvy, and the province, he says, is "supporting the dialogue."

The band is already taking water samples as part of Petrobank's environmental baseline assessment. "There is not a lot of employment here. Our youth are always

windows. I made notes on their health woes, their trouble getting physicians to take them seriously, and their feelings of abandonment. But none of these sources would agree to be identified by name.

In some cases, when potential whistleblowers edged towards going public with demands for compensation for health and property damage, companies were quick to offer cash settlements in exchange for signatures on non-disclosure agreements.

Others feared becoming embroiled in legal battles. Or they worried the bad publicity would cause their property values to plummet, blocking their exit and angering neighbours.

As one resident told me, "Look, I want to talk to you, but I've been shouting about this for five years, and no good has come of it. I can't afford to pay a lawyer. I just want to sell my land and get my family out of here."

Taken from a report in the Tyee March 23, 2004.

leaving to find work." Batini speaks quickly and passionately, fidgeting in his chair, crossing and uncrossing
his legs. "Who are these people that don't want us to do
this? Wealthy people who don't have to worry about
such things. Our land is the least developed in the
Okanagan — and now they don't want us to do this
because it's the last natural habitat left." What about
locals' claims that the 60-person band got a 25 percent
cut of the project in exchange for not opposing the
development? "There is no agreement to share revenue,"
he says.

While we had mainly been discussing Petrobank, I
later discovered that Vancouver-based Compliance
Energy has also purchased a smaller but still substantial
8,295-acre methane tenure in the area, with the Upper
Similkameen Indian Band a 25-percent partner. At the
same time, Compliance has another plan that is upsetting
many people in Princeton: to build a generating plant to
burn coal and sell the power to BC Hydro. If the company mixes some wood waste in with the coal, they meet
the B.C. Liberals' definition of "clean energy."

"We're walking a tightrope," Batini continues. "We are
both for economic development and for the environment. This industry is new to British Columbia. We are
very nervous, and we are learning as we go. We understand that the province will get hundreds of millions out
of this. Then there should be millions going into the local
economy, both for our band and the community as a
whole."

At the very least, Batini is leveraging his position. The
Princeton town council, on the other hand, has yet to
draw its line in the sand. "Council is not really decided
on the whole coal-bed methane thing, but I would like to
see us follow the line of the Concerned Citizens. They
want the environmental impacts reduced," mayor Keith

Olsen says, fingering a red flyer that announces a landowners' meeting for the following week. He wears a gold chain around his neck, and his short-sleeve plaid madras shirt is open a few buttons to reveal its gleam. He has deep lines of expression on his face when it's not in motion, like a man who spends a lot of time in the tropics. The only thing missing is the tan.

Olsen maintains that drilling for coalbed methane and the birth of tourism can coexist. He has recently been meeting with a planning committee to figure out how to promote the region. "Everybody's heard of the Okanagan, but who has heard of the Similkameen?" he says.

While he believes that the drilling will have some economic spillover from which Princeton hotels and restaurants will benefit, his optimism doesn't extend to the provincial government's claims of job opportunities. "All the companies will bring in their own crews, from Calgary or wherever," he says. "There will only be a few labourer type jobs, temporary ones like earth moving and road building, for locals."

How effectively does he feel the government has communicated with the town? "Sometimes, they are forthright with information, but they could have done more to be open to members of the community," he says. "But I imagine the government is gun shy after some of the public meetings they've had, where people are just screaming at them. When they came here, they didn't do an open Q&A meeting. They gave a presentation and had information kiosks. It was controlled."

The Regional District of Okanagan-Similkameen, of which he is a member, formally requested in July that the provincial government do an environmental assessment of coalbed methane before proceeding. "We brought up how their regulations and manpower had been cut, but the ministry people at the meeting said they were confident they had the staff to do this." The Oil and Gas Commission has taken on the assessment, which, as it is overseen by the Ministry of Energy and Mines, hardly seems like the most objective body, and the work has been delegated to Petrobank — ditto. "I think the community's concerns will be dealt with," Olsen responds. "Let's give the company the benefit of the doubt."

Drilling down property values

At dusk Paul Wylie stands on a dirt road that runs through the lodgepole pines on his hillside 100 acres. Just below him a mule deer and her fawn calmly graze on the grass in the gold and brown landscape. Below that is a level bench, deep green, where Wylie grows 16 acres of garlic and alfalfa, all organic. "I have a connection with the land, and most people don't anymore," he says. It is a picture-book farm, with old Massey Ferguson machinery settled here and there, and a log workshop — built by

FOREST OVERSIGHT BUZZSAWED

By **CHRIS TENOVE**

▪ Lyle Knight and his 34 colleagues at the Ministry of Forests (MOF) district office in Lillooet knew that cuts were coming. "When they announced that our office was closing," Knight says, "there were guys in their forties and fifties with tears streaming down their faces."

Eleven MOF district offices have closed in the last three years, including the one in Lillooet. The B.C. chapter of the Sierra Club of Canada released a report in December 2004 that totalled the MOF jobs lost: 800 in all, with 647 positions cut from smaller communities around the province. According to the report, nearly 40 percent of those cut were Scientific Technical Officers like Lyle Knight in Lillooet. These employees make up a large part of the Forest Service's compliance and enforcement staff.

At the same time that they have chopped away at the ranks

himself and his wife, as was his house — filled with perfect wooden birdhouses and feeders that he and a group of Katimavik students made.

In September, when he and his wife, Lauren Hamilton, first heard about the test well on Wright Road, they formed the group that caught the mayor's attention, Similkameen Citizens Concerned About Coal-Bed Methane. "The [provincial] government agenda is so strong, we decided not to ask them not to do it at all. We figured we wouldn't get anywhere. We're just asking them to do it right." Wylie has long wry features and straight strawman hair, graying. They have organized letters and petitions with hundreds of signatures that they sent to the provincial government. "It took two and a half months for Neufeld to answer our letter, and he sidestepped all our concerns." They have started to call the ministries themselves.

Because of the possibility of the water table dropping or being contaminated, he convinced the local organic

of the MOF, the Liberals have introduced an entirely new forestry regime. Forests minister Mike de Jong unveiled the Liberal "results-based" strategy in the fall of 2002. Now, government sets the sustainability objectives, but forest companies are given more flexibility to decide how to meet them. This shift is supposed to reduce the costs and "green tape" that industry encounters. The new legislation, called the Forest and Range Practices Act, took effect January 31, 2004.

But George Hoberg, head of the Department of Forest Resources Management at the University of British Columbia, cautions that industry may not take up Forest Service responsibilities.

'Offloaded' responsibilities

The new forestry strategy also shifts more responsibility onto professional foresters, who can now certify the plans made by private companies to log public

certifying body, Similkameen Okanagan Organic Producers Association, to make a resolution calling for a thor-
ough environmental assessment before there is any
coalbed methane development. He is working to get the
provincial certifying body to do the same. While his
property is not in the Petrobank tenure, many other
farms and ranches are. "Why do they have to do this on
agricultural land? I really have a problem with that. They
could at least restrict it to Crown land. Landowners
should have an option to say if they want it or not."

He is also worried about possible harm to what he sees
as the most promising new economy in the region. "People are just starting to come here because of the quality
of life, and this could ruin that," he says. "Land values in
the States in areas where they have done drilling have
gone down by up to 20 percent. Say your land is worth
$300,000 and you lease part of it to a drilling company
for $20,000 — but later, maybe you can't sell it at all.
People don't think of that."

FOREST OVERSIGHT [Cont.]

lands. Andrew Gage, a staff
lawyer with West Coast Environmental Law, argues that the
Liberal changes to forest practices are "part of a series of legislative changes that are
designed to offload government
responsibilities onto industry or
to private professionals hired by
industry."

Professional foresters are put
into an obvious conflict of
interest, says Gage. "Their jobs
are ultimately reliant on the forest companies," he says. "It's
unfair to continually put the
professional foresters in situations where they have to choose
between the public interest and
the desires of their actual
employer."

Back in 2001, an MOF investigation found that companies
were misleading the ministry in
their timber appraisals. That
same year, the Sierra Legal
Defence Fund released a report
on the industry practice and
estimated that it could have cost
the province $138 million over

It is dark now, and we go inside. His house is comfortably furnished, modern, with touches of craftsmanship he's probably done himself: picture frames constructed from old wine crates, a round clock cut from sheet metal, a lamp made from a slice of tree trunk. A friendly tabby purrs on a stool. "Every night Lauren and I go to bed and ask each other, 'Do you think we're making a difference?'" he says. "I think so. I think the government is only giving out information now because we are relentless. Of course, they're only giving out the message they want us to have. The schmoozers are out in full force." That wry look again.

"People say, 'I'm glad you're doing this.'" He sighs. "But then they won't help, their lives are too busy. This is a small community not focused on much but survival."

Just before I put on my boots to go into the rainy winter evening, Wylie says, "This is the thin edge of the wedge. They have lots of other locations planned. We have to set the benchmark here, get the regulations in

the previous 15-month period. In one case, according to a subsequent investigation by the *Vancouver Sun*, TimberWest paid only $22,700 for timber that was originally valued at $3.7 million.

Since then it has become even easier to mislead the MOF — according to the Sierra Club's 2004 report, cutbacks at MOF now mean that, on average, ministry scalers are able to examine just one out of every 147 truckloads of wood.

The Liberals' "results-based" approach shifts more responsibility onto private companies, and then rewards them by dramatically cutting back government oversight. A skeptic might wonder: if there are no MOF officials in the forest, does an improperly logged tree make a sound?

From an article published in the Tyee December 7, 2004.

place." He pauses and takes a deep breath, because there is more. He has come to realize that a groundswell of grassroots opposition is not enough in these times — it will take a landslide. "All over the province, people will have to tell the government to stuff it."

CHAPTER 6

Fiscal Fictions

By WILL MᶜMARTIN

MARK Twain was once asked by an aspiring novelist for the secret to writing popular fiction. "First you gather all your facts," he told Rudyard Kipling, "then you distort them as you can."

That dictum has been taken to heart by British Columbia's politicians over the past several decades, especially when the province's finances are concerned. Time and again, B.C.'s fiscal situation has been willfully distorted by premiers and finance ministers for their own political advantage.

No party has been immune to the affliction. W.A.C. Bennett once held a bond-burning ceremony on Lake Okanagan to celebrate B.C.'s freedom from debt. In reality, he had quietly shifted the government's financial obligations off Victoria's books and onto those of various provincial agencies. Then there was Bill Vander Zalm's Budget Stabilization Fund, described by critics as the "BS" fund, which later was shown to have been bare of cash.

The term "fudge-it budget" was popularized in the mid-1990s after the New Democratic Party government introduced two consecutive, pre-election budgets boasting razor-thin surpluses. Weeks after the NDP had won re-election, it was revealed that both touted surpluses had morphed into sizeable deficits.

Gathering the fiscal facts and distorting them has become a well-established political tactic in British Columbia, and Gordon Campbell's B.C. Liberals have carried on with the tradition. Mere days after winning the 2001 general election amid fulsome promises of honesty and accountability, the premier-designate baldly misrepresented the province's finances by portraying the massive surplus he had inherited from the defeated NDP as an enormous deficit.

The B.C. Liberals brought more than just a willingness to dissemble into government. The party's leading figures also embraced "supply-side" economics, a theory which posits that lower taxes stimulate increased economic activity, which in turn generates new revenues for government to offset losses from cutting taxes in the first place. Tax cuts, so it is said, "pay for themselves."

And so, within hours of taking power, and with the provincial treasury filled to overflowing, the Campbell government introduced gigantic tax cuts. At the same time, believing that tax cuts truly would pay for themselves, they also oversaw huge increases in public spending.

Instead of sparking economic growth, however, the combination of tax cuts and spending hikes generated horrendous deficits when B.C. followed the global economy into a downturn. As quickly as they had enacted their supply-side theory, the Campbell government abruptly reversed course, bringing in huge tax hikes and attempting to slash public expenditures.

In the grandest fiction of all, the B.C. Liberals claimed that this combination of tax cuts and spending increases, followed by tax increases and spending cuts, was all part of a master plan to produce a balanced budget in their third full fiscal year.

As if by magic, the balanced budget finally appeared in February 2004. Unmentioned by the B.C. Liberals and their supporters was the fact that they had taken office with a massive surplus in the provincial treasury, so had merely returned to whence they had started. Best forgotten, too, were the three giant deficits which preceded the sole balanced budget, and which added several billion dollars to British Columbia's debt.

Most importantly, there could be no mention that the reappearance of a budget surplus was due to massive transfer payments from the federal government, tax increases, medical premium hikes and soaring tuition fees. The tax cuts, it was plain to see if one chose to look, had failed to pay for themselves.

But in gathering the facts and then distorting them as they could, the B.C. Liberals claimed that British Columbia had "turned the corner" and "laid a firm foundation of good fiscal management" for future prosperity.

Fervently repeated by their supporters in the business community, this tale is well on its way to becoming conventional wisdom. It is pleasing to the ear, but just as false as B.C.'s debt-free status under W.A.C. Bennett, Vander Zalm's "B.S." fund, and the NDP's "fudge-it" budgets.

The opposite of conventional wisdom? Let's examine the Liberal record step by step.

Inside the binders

It was May 21, 2001. In the B.C. Parliament Buildings' west annex, home to the premier's office, two men in near-identical dark-blue suits stood before a gaggle of press gallery reporters. Five days earlier, British Columbia voters had delivered one of the most lopsided election verdicts in provincial history. Now, outgoing premier Ujjal Dosanjh met with Gordon Campbell to symbolically hand over the reins of power.

Arrayed on a table before the two party leaders were

seven large binders containing thousands of pages of briefing notes prepared by government bureaucrats. At one point Dosanjh playfully piled the binders, one at a time, high atop Campbell's outstretched arms. Yes, governing British Columbia can be an armful.

Later, Campbell reviewed the transition documents. The third binder, titled "Fiscal Situation," provided lengthy analyses of the government's finances and the B.C. economy. The information therein was far different from what British Columbians had been led to believe during the recent election campaign.

One of the concerns that caused voters to turf the New Democratic Party in 2001 was their mishandling of B.C.'s financial affairs. Elected to government in 1991, and narrowly re-elected in 1996, the NDP had delivered a seemingly never-ending series of annual operating deficits. These fiscal shortfalls, in turn, fed the near-constant growth of B.C.'s public debt.

The New Democrats had also enacted taxation measures which critics, notably the province's business community, charged were punitive for taxpayers and investors, and therefore harmful to the B.C. economy. Proof of these allegations seemed to lie in the province's anemic economic growth during the NDP's second term in office. After unspectacular but steady expansion for much of the decade following Expo '86, B.C.'s economy noticeably weakened in the latter half of the 1990s.

Worse, many voters believed the New Democrats had dishonestly misrepresented the government's finances. This perception was founded on two "balanced" budgets (for the fiscal years 1995-96 and 1996-97) which were introduced prior to the NDP government's re-election in 1996. After the election and the NDP victory, both fiscal plans — dubbed by critics "fudge-it budgets" — were revealed to be in deficit.

B.C.'s independent auditor general soon launched an investigation into the latter budget, taking testimony under oath from both elected politicians and senior bureaucrats. He later reported that "crucial information was missing" from the fiscal plan, which therefore contained "a disproportionate risk of being wrong on the downside." But he also found that the NDP government had complied with existing statutory requirements when preparing the budget. To prevent future recurrences, the auditor general called for "sweeping changes in how the budgeting process is governed by elected officials."

The NDP government gratefully accepted the suggestion of a statutory remedy, and appointed Douglas Enns, a Victoria accountant and businessman, to head a 12-member committee to recommend specific measures. In 2000, the panel's proposals were legislatively implemented in the Budget Transparency and Accountability Act.

Meanwhile, in B.C. Supreme Court, a small group of angry voters was claiming that the 1996 election had been won by fraudulent means. After lengthy legal wrangling, Justice Mary Humphries ruled that the plaintiffs' understanding of budget-making was "simplistic," found no evidence to support their claim, and dismissed the action. But the damage was done; many British Columbians saw the NDP as both incompetent and dishonest.

Ironically, as the NDP's second term in office drew to a close, the provincial economy began an unforeseen but stellar recovery. Where the annual growth rate (chained) of B.C.'s gross domestic product slumped in 1998 to a dismal 1.3 percent, in 1999 it jumped to a respectable 3.2 percent, and then in 2000 recorded an eye-popping 4.6 percent increase.

Together, B.C.'s improving economy and soaring energy receipts lifted government revenues to record levels. Where a deficit of $800 million in the consolidated revenue fund had been estimated in the 2000-01 budget (introduced in March 2000), a year later that shortfall was replace by a surplus initially pegged at an astounding $1.4 billion.

It was an amazing fiscal turn-around. Moreover, the finance ministry and an independent panel of economists forecast continued expansion in the coming fiscal year. Thus, in their 2001-02 budget, their 10th and last, the discredited New Democrats were able to accomplish two things. First, they hiked year-over-year spending by a whopping $1.8 billion, nearly all of which went to health, education and social services. Second, because soaring revenues provided a small surplus over expenditures, the budget was "balanced."

But little notice was given to B.C.'s improving fiscal situation and the incredible windfall accumulating in the

CONJURING A $5 BILLION 'NDP' DEFICIT

By WILL McMARTIN

■ Six weeks after announcing a "dramatic" 25-percent cut to B.C.'s personal income tax rates, premier Gordon Campbell received a 47-page report from the British Columbia Fiscal Review Panel. Appointed by Campbell on May 25, four days after he had received the briefing binders on government transition, the panel was asked to undertake "an independent review of the province's fiscal situation."

But the "independence" of the seven-member panel was open to question, as several participants, their companies or employers had made sizeable financial donations to the B.C. Liberal party. The review, moreover, was far less than the "comprehensive audit" Campbell had promised voters during the election campaign. Indeed, in its transmittal letter, the panel explicitly stated: "This is not an audit. We conducted the review by seeking information from the

provincial treasury. Instead, public attention was diverted by a startling accusation. The B.C. Liberals, losers in 1996 after two pre-election "fudge-it budgets," were loath to concede the fiscal high ground weeks before the 2001 contest, and finance critic Gary Collins was quickly on his feet after the 2001-02 budget was tabled in the legislature. "It's a real tragedy that this NDP government would once again present a false budget to the voters on the eve of an election," he said.

B.C. Hydro officials, Collins charged, had balked at making a $375 million dividend payment to Victoria, as required by the budget. This was puzzling insofar as Hydro had been contributing dividends since 1990. In recent years the average payment had been in excess of $400 million annually. Collins backed up his assertion with copies of pre-budget e-mails exchanged between the finance ministry and the Crown corporation.

The B.C. Liberal caucus promptly issued a news release with the headline, "They're doing it again: Fudge-it Bud-

professional public service and the public."

More than anything, Campbell's appointment of the panel followed an old political tradition in British Columbia, whereby newly-elected governments attempt to discredit their defeated predecessors for alleged fiscal incompetence and misconduct.

The pattern began in 1916, when the Conservative government lost to the Liberal opposition, the first time that a political party succeeded another in office. It occurred again in 1928, when the Tories regained power, and again in 1933, when the Liberals were restored to government.

The practice fell into abeyance for several decades, until the rejuvenated Social Credit party defeated Dave Barrett's New Democratic Party government in 1975. The Socreds retained the accounting firm of Clarkson Gordon to conduct an apparently "independent" review of

get 2." It claimed that by counting the disputed Hydro dividend as revenue, and improperly including a one-time pension plan adjustment, the NDP budget was not balanced, but in deficit by $310 million.

Business representatives enthusiastically entered the fray, but rather than praising the massive surplus recorded in 2000-01, or the balanced estimates for 2001-02, they sided with the B.C. Liberals. The B.C. Chamber of Commerce issued a news release which complained of "bloated government spending," "high taxes" and "accounting trickery." The chief economist at the Business Council of B.C., in a newspaper column, repeated many of the B.C. Liberal allegations but predicted an even-higher deficit, "in the vicinity of $1 billion."

There was no mention of the previous year's record-shattering surplus.

The tidal wave of accusations, most later proved false, continued unabated through the remainder of the legislative session and the subsequent election campaign. "As

CONJURING A DEFICIT [Cont.]

the province's books. That study pinpointed a number of items which, properly manipulated, could be used to retroactively suppress the outgoing government's revenues and boost its expenditures long after the New Democrats had been defeated.

The largest alteration centred on the Insurance Corporation of B.C. It had been launched by the NDP to provide mandatory automobile insurance to B.C. drivers, and as is the case with nearly all new companies, had

incurred significant start-up costs. Normally these expenditures would be carried on the company's books as debt and amortized over time. But the Socreds decided to pay down the entire debt immediately out of the consolidated revenue fund, thereby creating a one-time, unbudgeted expenditure of $175 million that was added to the deficit left by the defeated New Democrats.

Sixteen years later, the NDP exacted their revenge when they

everyone now knows, the NDP's 1996 election budget was a fraud," declared the B.C. Liberals' election platform. "Now they are at it again. The NDP's new budget has been exposed as yet another 'fudge-it budget.'"

These allegations of fiscal shenanigans resonated with the voting public, and the New Democratic Party was all but wiped out at the polls. Left unanswered, however, were questions concerning the province's finances, and the most important was: What were the real numbers?

'Worse than we thought'

The answers were in the transition binders given to Campbell (obtained by this writer through a Freedom of Information request) after the election. In the third binder, prepared by finance ministry bureaucrats, was an update accounting of provincial finances since the NDP budget had been introduced three months earlier. The numbers confirmed the strength of B.C.'s economy, and the astonishing transformation of the province's fiscal situation.

hired the firm of Peat Marwick after defeating the Socreds in the 1991 provincial general election. Measures taken by the New Democrats to retroactively boost the Socreds' deficit included rejecting a budgeted $250 million B.C. Hydro dividend (thereby reducing revenues by that same amount), and incurring new expenditures of more than $300 million by "writing off" outstanding loans to businesses and students. In total, the New Democrats were able to increase the Socred deficit by more than six hundred million dollars.

In 2001 the newly-elected B.C. Liberal government spurned private-sector accounting firms, and instead hand-picked a "cross-section of representatives from the business community." Heading the panel was Gordon Barefoot, a chartered accountant who had served on a similar body in Alberta in 1993. Then living in Edmonton, he was appointed by Alberta finance

For the fiscal year just ended (2000-01), the surplus in the consolidated revenue fund was forecast at nearly $1.4 billion — an increase of $85 million over the NDP budget. Net income for B.C.'s Crown corporations was now pegged at $185 million — a gain of $21 million. And since the "forecast allowance" hadn't been used, another $150 million automatically went to the bottom line.

(The "forecast allowance" is a line-item expense in the annual budget — specifically in the summary accounts — at the beginning of a fiscal year, even though there are no formal plans to spend it. It is in the budget to acknowledge that there may be unforeseen rises in expenditure, or shortfalls in revenues, and is also known as a "contingency," "fiscal cushion" or "fudge factor." The forecast allowance was one of a number of budget-making reforms introduced by the NDP following the fudge-it budget scandal, first appearing as a "revenue allowance" in the 1999-2000 budget before gaining its current appellation in 2000-01.)

CONJURING A DEFICIT [Cont.]

minister Jim Dinning to a nine-member panel after Ralph Klein's election as premier. Paul Taylor, then an aide to Dinning, later a senior adviser to the B.C. Liberals, helped to recruit Barefoot after the latter moved to Vancouver to work with BC Gas.

Barefoot and his panel colleagues faced a unique challenge, however, a situation different from that presented to Clarkson Gordon in 1975 or Peat Marwick in 1991 when those firms helped their clients to dis-

credit the previous government. In both those instances, the newly-elected Social Credit and NDP governments had taken power with just a few months remaining in the current fiscal year. In other words, they had sufficient time to make significant revenue or expenditure decisions to the budgets left by their defeated predecessors before year-end.

But the B.C. Liberals took office at the beginning of June 2001, just two months into the

Consequently, the surplus in the overall summary accounts was $1.573 billion — a $256-million improvement from the NDP's revised forecast for the previous year. And the binder also offered an analysis of the current period's budget figures: although still early in the fiscal year, "the summary accounts are projected to be in balance in 2001-02."

In short, the final NDP budget had understated the surplus from 2000-01, and accurately portrayed the estimates for 2001-02. The auditor general's report and the Enns' committee's recommendations had served their purpose: budget preparation and presentation had improved considerably. And, as an added bonus, British Columbia's fiscal situation had strengthened because the provincial economy was firing on all cylinders. The public debt had been reduced, the budget was balanced, and the treasury filled to overflowing.

One might think that the newly elected Campbell government had found itself in an enviable fiscal position.

new fiscal year. The books for 2000-01 were closed, and under audit. They could not be retroactively altered. Even worse for the new government, when the 2000-01 public accounts were made public, they would show that the defeated NDP had left the biggest surplus in B.C. history. It would not be possible for the incoming Campbell government to claim that they had inherited a deficit from the New Democrats based on audited financial statements.

Moreover, fiscal 2001-02 was already underway, but the budget estimates had not been passed. The NDP had enacted an "interim supply" bill which provided funds only until the end of July. The Campbell government, therefore, would have to obtain legislative approval to spend monies for the balance of the fiscal year. It would be difficult, if not impossible, to plausibly claim that the NDP had created a massive deficit when they had been in power for mere

But the rosy picture painted by the third briefing binder presented a political dilemma of sorts. After all, the B.C. Liberals' election victory in part rested on the assertion that the New Democrats' final budget was in deficit and "fudged." The briefing binders clearly showed those allegations to be untrue, a revelation that might prove embarrassing for the new government.

Yet, the B.C. Liberals' election platform had promised to "deliver real transparent, accountable government." With pledges such as these, surely the new premier had no choice but to accurately disclose the binders' contents to the public. Or did he?

Two days after the transition ceremony, in a scrum with press gallery reporters at Victoria's Empress Hotel where the 77-member B.C. Liberal caucus was holding its first post-election meeting, Gordon Campbell gave his answer. "Some of the problems that we face are as we thought and some are worse than we thought," he said, "The finances of the province are worse than we antici-

CONJURING A DEFICIT [Cont.]

weeks in fiscal 2001-02, and the B.C. Liberals for the remaining 10 months.

The Barefoot panel found an innovative solution to this dilemma. Unable to manufacture a New Democratic Party deficit for the past or the present, they skillfully projected a massive shortfall for the future. In other words, they ignored the previous fiscal year, 2000-01, and the current year, 2001-02, and instead created a NDP deficit for 2003-04 — three years after the

New Democrats had been defeated.

Barefoot and his panel colleagues started with the consolidated revenue fund. They took a three-year forecast from the NDP's 2001-02 budget, and cut revenues by about $1 billion while raising expenditures by about $1.5 billion. So, where the NDP's three-year forecast showed a balanced budget in 2003-04, the Barefoot panel had created a $2.52 billion deficit. They called this a 'status quo'

pated." He added, "The magnitude of the losses we may face compared to budget is still up in the air."

Banner headlines in the following day's daily newspapers fairly screamed that the defeated New Democrats had left behind a fiscal mess for the new government. "B.C. Finances Worse Than Thought, Campbell Says," blared the *Vancouver Sun*.

Five weeks later, without fanfare, B.C.'s public accounts for fiscal 2001-02 were released by the comptroller general and auditor general. They confirmed record-shattering surpluses in the consolidated revenue fund and the summary accounts. So great was the fiscal windfall that British Columbia was able to make its largest-ever reduction to the public debt. When Gordon Campbell and the B.C. Liberals took office, the provincial debt stood at $33.8 billion, down $616 million from the previous year.

Far from inheriting a fiscal disaster from the NDP, Campbell and his party were given a provincial treasury

---

forecast, because it ignored the possibility that the provincial government could or would alter expenditures, or change taxes or other revenues over the intervening years.

They then turned to the "forecast allowance." As detailed earlier in this chapter, this device had been introduced to provincial budgets in the late 1990s to act as a fiscal "cushion," not meant to be spent, but counted as an expenditure at the beginning of the fiscal year in case of a potential shortage in revenues or an unplanned expense during the period. In 2000-01, the budget had a forecast allowance of $300 million, but it was unspent because of the massive surplus. NDP forecast allowances were about 1.25 percent of consolidated revenue fund expenditures, but Barefoot argued that the forecast should be 4.5 percent in fiscal 2003-04, or $1.25 billion.

From these two sources, the consolidated revenue fund alter-

brimming with cash. But the voting public was led to think very much otherwise.

Born-again tax cutter

The B.C. Liberals probably would have won the 2001 general election with or without making a great many campaign promises, so deep was the animus voters felt for the NDP. But Gordon Campbell and his colleagues committed themselves to a vast array of initiatives, including a controversial pledge to enact a "dramatic" cut to personal income tax rates.

Two points are noteworthy about this promise. First, it rested on the belief that British Columbia's economy and the province's finances started to deteriorate only after the New Democrats took power in 1991. According to this line of reasoning, propagated by business interests, the NDP had raised taxes and B.C. subsequently descended into a 'dismal decade' of economic stagnation and government deficits.

CONJURING A DEFICIT [Cont.]

ations ($2.52 billion) and the revised forecast allowance ($1.25 billion), Barefoot was able to create a deficit of more than $3.75 billion which would appear three years into the future.

Incredibly, to this manufactured shortfall was added another $1.5 billion representing the revenues lost as a result of the B.C. Liberals' cuts in personal income tax rates. In effect, the defeated New Democrats were blamed for the deficit which would arise from B.C. Lib-

eral tax cuts! The total deficit which the Barefoot panel attributed to to the defeated New Democrats was a massive $5.27 billion.

The Vancouver Sun once again obliged with a supportive headline: "B.C. risks $5-billion in 3 years." Over the next several years, a frequent refrain would arise from Gordon Campbell, Gary Collins and other B.C. Liberals over the massive deficit they "inherited" from the NDP.

Second, it raised questions about Gordon Campbell's personal commitment to tax reduction. As mayor of Vancouver and chair of the Greater Vancouver Regional District, Campbell had continually increased public expenditures while appearing indifferent to the plight of taxpayers. Only after sitting on the opposition benches in Victoria did he become a champion of smaller government and lower taxes.

A little history is useful in examining both points. From the end of the Second World War until the early 1980s, British Columbia's economy expanded rapidly as natural resources were exported to fast-growing markets in the United States and Japan. Government expenditures increased at an astounding pace, but revenues rose even faster, and were sufficient to generate near-continual fiscal surpluses.

Stability was the hallmark of provincial politics over the 30-year period between 1952 and 1982. The Social Credit party, led first by W.A.C. Bennett and later by his son, Bill, formed the government for nearly 27 years, with the New Democrats (and their fore-runners, the CCF) as the official opposition. For the remaining three years, 1972-75, the roles were reversed: the NDP was in government and the Socreds in opposition.

But in 1982, B.C. was hit by its second-worst economic recession since the Great Depression of the 1930s. Afterward, the provincial economy experienced halting, uneven growth, interrupted frequently by global uncertainty. Fiscal deficits became the norm, as the consolidated revenue fund showed just four surpluses in 20 years. The public debt seemed to grow at an ever-increasing rate.

Political change became the order of the day. Social Credit fell from power in 1991, and within a few years disappeared completely from the Legislative Assembly.

Ten years later, the defeated New Democratic Party found itself in a similar position, its future uncertain. Discomfited and disillusioned by two decades of economic and fiscal decline accompanied by ongoing political scandals, B.C. voters rejected the two parties which for a half-century had dominated their province. In 2001, the inexperienced, untested B.C. Liberal party was handed the biggest legislative majority in provincial history.

Gordon Campbell was British Columbia's eighth premier in 15 short years. He appeared unconcerned, and perhaps was unaware, of the province's postwar economic and fiscal history. To the exclusion of all other factors, the B.C. Liberal leader seemed focused solely on the "dismal decade," the period during the 1990s when the NDP was in government. And he offered a simple remedy to cure British Columbia's ills: tax cuts.

But the image Campbell presented to B.C. voters — of himself as a champion for beleaguered taxpayers and an advocate for smaller, more affordable government — sharply contrasted with his lengthy record in civic politics. When it came to taxes and size of government, he was a politician transformed.

From 1986 to 1992, as mayor of Vancouver, he presided over a rise in the cost of salaries and benefits for municipal employees from $214.6 million to $341 million — a 59 percent increase. Administrative costs rose from $17.2 million to $24.5 million — up nearly 44 percent. In total, Vancouver's annual expenditures soared from $324.5 million to $498 million — a hike of 53 percent.

These dizzying spending hikes were accompanied by tax increases that proved increasingly burdensome for city homeowners and local business proprietors. The average Vancouver property tax bill during Campbell's first six years as mayor skyrocketed by nearly 68 percent. Eventually, irate business owners in the Kerrisdale neighbourhood formed the Angry Taxpayers' Action Committee (ATAC) to protest the mayor's seeming indifference to their plight. "In our struggle to keep afloat over the past years," ATAC secretary-treasurer Alexa Allen wrote in a letter to a local newspaper, "he [Campbell] has shown no initiative or compassion to solve the problems we face with high taxes."

It was a similar situation at the Greater Vancouver Regional District, chaired by Campbell from 1991 to 1993. A GVRD finance report showed that under his stewardship the district recorded its three biggest spending increases, ever. Asked to comment by the news media, the Vancouver mayor absolved himself: "I cannot take responsibility for all these costs," he said.

But in the spring of 1993, then entering his seventh year as mayor, Gordon Campbell was politically reborn. The metamorphosis began when NDP premier Mike Harcourt's government introduced a property surtax which was expected to raise $37 million annually. Levied on residences valued at $500,000 and above, the surtax angered homeowners on Vancouver's affluent west side.

This was understandable, for municipal taxes on the average west-side residence had shot up from $984 to $1,702 per year during Campbell's first six years as mayor — an increase of 73 percent. (The cost-of-living index had risen by just 27 percent over that same period.) Many west-side homeowners felt that the NDP government's proposed levy was an unbearable addition to their already onerous municipal tax burden.

The Vancouver mayor joined with other Lower Mainland mayors in organizing protest rallies against the NDP surtax on property. As anger mounted, Harcourt, himself a west-side resident and deluged with complaints from neighbours and friends, ordered the property levy killed. Undeterred by victory, Campbell went ahead with a planned protest at the Oakridge Mall, where he roused an estimated 5,000 protestors with these words: "I'm not willing to let any government tax away my dreams."

Almost overnight, Gordon Campbell's image was remade. Where once had stood a free-spending, high-taxing municipal politician, there now was a fierce defender of besieged provincial taxpayers. Before the year was over, he had become leader of the B.C. Liberal party.

Taking his seat in the Legislative Assembly in 1994, Campbell's maiden legislative speech was a blistering attack on NDP taxation policies. "This government creates uncertainty at every turn," he thundered. "It taxes investment in job creation and calls it a corporate capital tax. It imposes on small businesses the highest tax rate of any jurisdiction in Canada. It establishes the highest marginal income tax rate in Canada."

New Democratic Party MLAs were incredulous at Campbell's about-face. "When we look at the record, let's not forget," cabinet minister Moe Sihota told the House, "that when the leader of the opposition was mayor of Vancouver, taxes for small business went up by 62 percent." Harcourt, too, entered the fray. The B.C. Liberal leader, while mayor, had "increased the city of Vancouver's accumulated debt by 46 percent," he said.

Campbell appeared unperturbed by these attacks, and his rightward journey across the political spectrum was clearly illustrated in The Courage to Change, the B.C. Liberals' policy platform for the 1996 provincial general election. To meet his promise of a "smaller and smarter government," the platform outlined three specific tax cuts: a 15 percent reduction in personal income taxes, abolition of the corporation capital tax, and the gradual elimination of the school tax on property.

Provincial revenues were expected to decline as a result

of these tax rollbacks, so it was necessary to trim the cost of government by 15 percent over four years. Among other measures, the platform proposed chopping the Legislative Assembly to "less than 60 MLAs", rolling-back the number of government ministries and cabinet ministers from 18 to 12, and privatizing government-owned BC Rail.

But to many voters, the numbers simply did not add up. Pundits and political opponents calculated the 15 percent reduction in the size of government meant that as much as $3 billion in government spending would have to be slashed to meet Campbell's goal of a balanced budget. Campbell himself came under fire for his chameleon-like transformation from a big-spending, high-taxing municipal politician to a provincial fiscal hawk, and for making an hilarious attempt to connect with blue-collar and rural voters by ditching his business suit for a plaid workshirt.

Voters were unconvinced by the performance. Despite heading into the campaign with a comfortable lead in public opinion polls, the B.C. Liberals emerged on election day with just 33 seats, six fewer than the 39 won by the NDP under its new leader, Glen Clark. Campbell returned to the opposition benches as the New Democrats embarked on a second term in government.

Cuts without pain?

Five years later, as Campbell and the B.C. Liberals prepared their second election platform, A New Era for British Columbia, some key adjustments were made to soothe voters who might lack courage for the pain tax cuts could cause.

True, the New Era echoed The Courage to Change by pledging mandatory balanced budgets and the elimination of the corporation capital tax. And cuts to personal income tax rates remained a platform centrepiece — but with a twist. In 1996, the B.C. Liberals had vowed to slash income taxes by a specific amount, 15 percent. The New Era merely promised "a dramatic cut."

As described in the 2001 platform, a Campbell government would slice B.C.'s personal income tax rates for the bottom two of five tax brackets to "the lowest rate of any province in Canada . . . within our first term." In effect, the promise was to cut income taxes for residents earning $60,000 per year or less by an unspecified amount at some point over the next four years. Campbell demurred when asked by reporters to estimate the size of his tax cuts. "My goal is to make it as dramatic as possible," he said.

Moreover, the B.C. Liberal leader declared, "It would be irresponsible for me to suggest what that tax cut will be until I know what the status of the books are." The New Era platform, therefore, promised "a comprehensive audit of the Province's finances within 90 days" after the election.

The dodge enabled Campbell to avoid repeating a key mistake from 1996. Then, the 15 percent income tax reduction was offset by an identical 15 percent decrease in government spending so as to balance the budget, a tacit acknowledgment that tax cuts had a cost. By 2001, the Campbell Liberals knew that linking tax cuts with reductions in government expenditures was a losing electoral proposition. The promise of an independent financial audit, therefore, provided convenient political cover.

To further sweeten the pot, the 2001 platform, in contrast to its 1996 predecessor, pledged to maintaining health and education spending at then-current levels, with future increases dependent upon the growth of B.C.'s economy.

The New Era also excised all 1996 references to downsizing the public sector or selling government assets. There was no mention of cutting the cost of government by 15 percent, or reducing the number of MLAs to 60 or fewer, or appointing a cabinet of no more than a dozen portfolios. The most noticeable change concerned BC Rail: far from proposing to sell it, the Campbell Liberals now explicitly vowed to "not sell or privatize" the Crown corporation.

Indeed, the few token references in the New Era to reducing "the cost of government" illustrated how desperately the B.C. Liberals wanted to avoid a debate over possible reductions in public expenditures. They merely suggested that economies might be found through such painless measures as "increasing efficiencies" and "eliminating wasteful spending on government propaganda."

There even were a few proposals to increase spending so as to reduce wasteful expenditures. The auditor general, for example, was promised additional funding "to help identify and prevent waste," and a "Waste Buster" website would be developed for public input.

Another example of the B.C. Liberals' kinder, gentler approach to slashing taxes was the promised timetable for balancing the budget. In The Courage to Change, the date was set firmly at two years, come hell or high water. In New Era, this objective was pushed back to the third "full" fiscal year. In other words, a Campbell government would rely on deficit budgets almost until it was time to face voters again.

The business community, surprisingly, supported the assumed deficits, as was made clear when representatives from the BC Business Summit visited the *Vancouver Sun*'s editorial board. "If you have a situation that needs to go through a transition, a transformation, and you have a plan to do that, and that plan includes deficit spending to get there," said Jeff Mooney, owner of A&W Restaurants and chair of the summit, "then I think that is acceptable." It was a far cry from businesses' constant carping about red ink during the 1990s when the NDP was in power.

But all of these reversals paled in comparison to one other: Campbell now claimed that tax cuts had no cost. In 1996 he had admitted that tax cuts required off-setting spending reductions so as to ensure a balanced budget; now, in 2001, he argued that tax cuts would pay for themselves.

This assertion, based on "supply-side" economic theory, led to one of the sharpest and most entertaining political contretemps in B.C. during recent years. The exchange did not involve the New Democrats or their supporters from organized labour. Rather, it pitted the B.C. Liberals against David Bond, a respected economist at HSBC Bank Canada.

In January 2001, Bond spoke at an economic outlook conference hosted by the Vancouver Board of Trade and noted troubling signs in B.C.'s two largest export markets. The economy in the United States appeared to be slowing after robust growth in the 1990s, while Japan's recovery from a decade-long recession was uncertain. Bond advised his audience that Gordon Campbell and the B.C. Liberals, if elected to government, should avoid making "dramatic" tax cuts because their beneficial impact would be overwhelmed by the negative impact of decreasing demand in the U.S. and Asia. In that event, B.C.'s lower taxes would merely ensure a decline in government revenues and create sizeable deficits. The only way to avoid fiscal disaster was to make deep spending cuts, but in Bond's opinion, Campbell did not have "the stomach" for it.

Gary Collins, the B.C. Liberals' finance critic, defended his leader. "History has proved him wrong," he said, firing back at Bond. "In every jurisdiction in Canada which has reduced personal income tax rates in the last five to six years there has been no significant drop-off [in revenues] and the ones that have cut the most, like Alberta and Ontario, have seen the biggest increases in revenues."

It was a tricky situation for the HSBC bank's president, Martin Glynn, who had attended a hockey game with Collins the same day that Bond's comments were reported in the news media. Collins later admitted that he had complained to Glynn about Bond's remarks, and the economist's contract with the bank was abruptly terminated.

It was an entertaining sideshow to the real battle between the governing New Democrats and the B.C. Liberals. The contrast between the two major parties was made even clearer by NDP premier Dosanjh: "If you want tax cuts," he said in a televised speech to the province before the election, "I'm not your man."

In contrast, Gordon Campbell offered so-called free tax cuts following a comprehensive audit of the government's books. Public spending would not be reduced, deficit financing would continue for at least three years, and tax cuts would, it was claimed, pay for themselves. It was an easy choice for many B.C. voters.

A summer to remember

The summer of 2001 will be long remembered in B.C.'s fiscal history. On two separate days, June 6 and July 30, the newly elected B.C. Liberal government announced massive tax reductions which quickly produced a series of gargantuan deficits and added billions of dollars to the province's debt.

On the first date, exactly three weeks after the B.C. Liberals won the biggest legislative majority in provincial history, Gordon Campbell held a news conference to deliver his election promise of "dramatic" cuts to personal income tax rates. Beside him was Gary Collins, the new finance minister.

It was their first official day of work. Twenty-four hours earlier, the B.C. Liberal cabinet had been introduced at Government House. Observers were surprised at the cabinet's size, the biggest in provincial history. In 1996 Campbell had promised to reduce the executive council to just 12 portfolios. Now, five years later, 28 ministers took the oath of office.

There were 20 line-department ministers, seven junior ministers of state and the premier, all of whom required political staff, offices, automobiles and other expensive infrastructure. As was the case at Vancouver city hall and the GVRD, Campbell seemed predisposed to enlarging the size and cost of his own administrative empire.

The selection of Collins to head the finance department was not unexpected. Still, some found his appointment curious, given his credentials. Born and raised in Saskatchewan, Collins moved to B.C. hoping to become a pilot with the Canadian Armed Forces. Rejected for medical reasons, he later obtained a college aviation diploma and was hired as a flight instructor. He also married his first wife, Carmen Farrell, adding her name to his own, took an interest in provincial politics, and was instrumental in Campbell's rise within the B.C. Liberal party.

The B.C. Liberal finance critic who preceded Collins was Fred Gingell, a businessman and founder of Mohawk Oil. Gingell held the post for eight years, and earned respect from both sides in the legislature as well as from B.C.'s business community. When he passed away in June 1999, Campbell named Farrell-Collins as his successor. In effect, he decided to replace a 69-year old chartered accountant with a 36-year old flight instructor whose sole business experience consisted of working in a restaurant. But Farrell-Collins showed unquestioning loyalty to his party leader, as well as a flair for attacks on NDP cabinet ministers.

In 2001, divorced from his first wife and minus her surname, Collins was elected to his third term in the Legislative Assembly. And when the B.C. Liberal cabinet was introduced, he was assigned the demanding finance portfolio.

A day after taking the oath of office, and shortly following the B.C. Liberals' first cabinet meeting, Campbell and Collins briefed press gallery reporters. "The first order of business at cabinet's inaugural meeting today," said Campbell, "was ensuring British Columbians take more of their paycheques home each month." Personal income tax rates, he declared, had been cut across the board by an average of 25 percent.

British Columbians in all five income brackets received the tax reduction, not just the bottom two as promised during the election campaign. According to finance department calculations, an individual earning $20,000 per year would see their annual provincial tax bill decline by $236. A person with a yearly income of $80,000 would save $1,947 per annum.

Some observers quibbled about the decision to extend the tax cuts to all taxpayers, and not just those in the bottom two brackets, but the dramatic announcement was generally well received by the news media.

Few questions were raised about the cost of the measure, estimated by finance department officials at $1.5 billion annually. This was more than six percent of Victoria's yearly revenues, and represented a sizeable hole to be filled either with new sources of income or reduced expenditures. Or could a tax cut that big really pay for itself?

Collins assured everyone that it would. "The antidote has worked in other provinces." And he repeated the fiction that British Columbia's economic and fiscal difficulties had started in the 1990s, saying that "quick and decisive action" was needed "to turn around the decade of economic malaise that has plagued B.C."

But a glaring point was ignored by the news media and pundits: the B.C. Liberals had not conducted the promised "comprehensive audit" before making the tax cuts. Indeed, during the election campaign Campbell said it would be "irresponsible" to slash personal income tax rates without first examining B.C.'s books. Now, barely 24 hours after being sworn into office, he did exactly that.

Without a financial audit, the only documents available to Campbell, Collins and their colleagues were the final NDP budget (called "fudge-it budget 2" by the B.C. Liberals) and the seven briefing binders provided by Dosanjh on May 21. As related earlier, the third binder

SECRET CONTRACT WITH TARNISHED U.S. FIRM

By SCOTT DEVEAU

■ In its move to privatize PharmaCare and the Medical Service Plan, the provincial government hired a company that was found by the state of Wisconsin to have misappropriated public funds.

The same company, Virginia-based Maximus Ltd., has been embroiled in controversies in four other states, involving accusations of mismanagement, overspending or improperly receiving information while seeking a contract.

On November 4, 2004, the provincial government signed a ten-year, $324-million contract with the Canadian subsidiaries of Maximus to run the province's Medical Services Plan and PharmaCare programs.

Outsourcing services to American firms has raised concerns about whether the Patriot Act opens B.C. medical records to U.S. intelligence agencies. Minister of Health Colin Hansen assured the province there is nothing to worry about.

showed that the B.C. Liberals had inherited a record fiscal surplus and a reduced public debt.

In 1996, Campbell had proposed to lower personal income taxes by 15 percent, and was rejected by voters worried over the cost of the promise. Five years later, he delivered a whopping reduction of 25 percent. Could the burgeoning provincial treasury have persuaded the B.C. Liberals to make a "dramatic" $1.5-billion tax cut merely because the briefing binder indicated they could afford to do so?

And did the briefing binder also dissuade Campbell from ordering the promised financial audit? When asked by reporters about the contents of the transition binders, he had starkly misrepresented B.C.'s fiscal situation, saying they were "worse" than expected. Was Campbell fearful that a comprehensive and independent audit would vindicate the defeated New Democrats?

Whatever the reason, the Campbell government had made a $1.5-billion policy decision after being in power

---

But here in B.C., not much scrutiny has fallen on Maximus's corporate history of handling public funds. The company, which is one of the largest providers of outsourced business and information technology to governments, has 280 offices in the U.S., Canada, Puerto Rico and the Virgin Islands and more than 5000 employees worldwide. It provides a range of services from welfare, educational and judicial programs, to debt collection on student loans and child support.

In fact, Maximus runs B.C.'s Family Maintenance Enforcement Program through its subsidiary Themis Ltd., a company that has enforced child support payments in the province since 1988. Maximus bought out Themis in 2002.

The Medical Services Plan and PharmaCare contracts were put out to tender in 2003. Only one Canadian firm, CGI, was in contention, and Maximus put together the best proposal, according to the Ministry of Health.

for less than 24 hours, and without a formal audit. It was one of the costliest decisions ever seen in Victoria.

Eight weeks later, on July 30, Collins unveiled additional tax reductions in the Legislative Assembly. The occasion was the delivery of an "economic and fiscal update" — in effect, a "mini-budget" — to obtain legislative authority for expenditures in fiscal 2001-02.

(The NDP government had introduced a budget before the general election, but the spending estimates were not passed by the legislature. Instead, an interim supply bill provided monies for four months, or until the end of July. In order for the B.C. Liberals to obtain spending authority for the remaining eight months of the fiscal year, the legislature had to reconvene before August.)

Where the earlier tax cuts were directed to individuals, businesses now gained relief. The corporation capital tax on non-financial institutions was eliminated over a two-year period at a loss for the treasury of $273 million in a full fiscal year. The corporate sales tax rate was sliced

SECRET CONTRACT [Cont.]

But Maximus has stumbled out of the gates when entering other new territories. In Wisconsin, 10 months into Maximus's contract, out of the 1,100 clients who were supposed to have work placement assignments, only 507 had received them, and just 88 were actually participating, according to *New York Times* reporter Jason DeParle, who wrote a book about the welfare system in Wisconsin, excerpted in the *Washington Monthly*.

Maximus had other problems, DeParle noted. Caseworkers were handling more than twice the caseload allowed under state rules; at least two caseworkers were addicted to crack and another was hospitalized with job-related stress; and some caseworkers were caught pressuring welfare recipients for sex and drugs.

Rowland told the Tyee that Maximus was very disappointed in DeParle's article. "It's not necessarily that it was inaccurate.

three percentage points to 13.5 percent, with an annual loss of $200 million. Manufacturing machinery and equipment was exempted from the sales tax, thereby lowering yearly government revenues by $160 million. These and a few other minor measures meant the provincial treasury would forego $628 million each full fiscal year.

Combined, the June 6 personal income tax cuts and the July 30 business tax reductions meant an annual loss of more than $2.1 billion for the provincial treasury.

A prudent government at this point might have considered offsetting these sizeable revenue losses with comparable reductions in expenditure. In other words, an administration seeking to balance its budget would have cut spending by an amount equal to the reduction in revenues.

This was not the path taken by the B.C. Liberals. Instead, they did the polar opposite as Collins' mini-budget actually boosted government spending by an

---

The parts excerpted in the *Washington Monthly* are some of the more salacious elements of the book," Rowland said.

"Management and some judgment, in retrospect, probably were not the best, but it was a very unusual circumstance. It was one of the first outsourced welfare programs."

Government audit found misspending

In addition to the inner turmoil, a legislative audit found Max-imus billed Wisconsin taxpayers for more than $400,000 in questionable and unallowable expenses and an additional $1.6 million in expenses that lacked sufficient documentation for reimbursement.

The legislative audit prompted State Representative Mark Pocan to name Maximus the July 2000 Golden Turkey, awarded to the worst bill, agency action or political development each month in Wisconsin.

Maximus has fixed the situa-

amount which exceeded the revenues lost through his tax cuts.

The New Democrats' pre-election budget contained an enormous $1.8 billion increase in spending over the previous fiscal year. But lacking legislative approval, these planned expenditures could easily have been reversed or tossed aside by the massive B.C. Liberal majority.

Yet Collins not only accepted the NDP expenditures, he added another $455 million in new outlays. The year-over-year spending increase outlined in Collins' mini-budget was almost $2.3 billion — a gigantic 12.1 percent increase over the previous fiscal year.

To many, it was bewildering. In power for just two months, Gordon Campbell, Gary Collins and their B.C. Liberal colleagues had slashed yearly revenues by $2.1 billion, and raised annual government spending by $2.3 billion.

To Collins, it all made sense. "Already people are seeing our province in a new light," he boasted in the legisla-

SECRET CONTRACT [Cont.]

tion, and the welfare program they continue to run today in Wisconsin has become a model to be used in other states, Rowland said. In the end, Maximus agreed to pay back $500,000 to the state and an additional $500,000 to community organizations in Milwaukee County.

Controversies and accusations have surfaced in other states, as well. In Florida, where Maximus ran the child support program, the *Tallahassee Democrat* newspaper reported that the company

was overcharging for some services. Maximus's Rowland denies any wrongdoing, but the company ended its contract early.

In Colorado, Maximus's contract was discontinued after the state received 3000 complaints from people dependent on the company's services.

Leslie Wolfe, the B.C. government's executive contract manager on the Maximus deal, said she is confident none of these problems will occur here because of the "comprehensive

ture. "Business confidence is up, and so is consumer confidence." Then he offered a bold forecast. "We believe this confidence will translate into growth of 3.8 percent in our economy next year." Tax cuts, he said, "will allow businesses to once again create jobs, compete and attract investment. They send a message — that B.C. is back and ready to lead again."

B.C.'s business community was surprised and delighted by Collins' tax reductions. "I expected something, but I didn't expect tax cuts on quite that scale," said Jock Finlayson of the Business Council of B.C. "I guess if there's a surprise it's that the menu of tax reductions for business is as complete as it is," added Dave Park of the Vancouver Board of Trade. At the BC Chamber of Commerce, John Winter enthused that Collins' tax cuts not only would pay for themselves, but would do so quickly. "I think the economy is going to improve much more radically than he's predicting," he said.

The sudden and unexpected appearance of multi-bil-

---

contract" they have in place.

The contract, which was not made public because of Maximus's proprietary concerns, is a flat fee which precludes overspending. If Maximus goes over budget, the difference comes out of its own pocket, Wolfe said.

Conflict of interest clauses stipulate that if Maximus is found influencing subsequent contracts or making political contributions, the contract will be terminated, according to Wolfe, who adds that Maximus is also subject to annual audits.

"What happened in Wisconsin was a great learning experience. There was no intention to do anything wrong and in fact the [Wisconsin] Attorney General said there was no criminal intent, that this was just bad bookkeeping," Rowland told the Tyee. She added: "We're very much excited about working in British Columbia."

From a report published by the Tyee December 3, 2004.

lion dollar deficits in fiscal 2001-02 did not seem to concern the business community. Where the NDP budget for the year had forecast a modest $290 million surplus in the consolidated revenue fund, and a "zero" balance in the summary accounts (before accounting for the forecast allowance and joint trusteeship of government pension plans), the B.C. Liberals' mini-budget showed shortfalls of $2.0 billion and $2.3 billion respectively.

But out-of-province commentators were less restrained. "Somewhat optimistic," was how a TD Economics report described Collins' forecast of 3.8 percent GDP growth in the coming year. The bank's economists fretted about what it would take to ever balance the budget. With fine fiscal understatement, the report noted the necessary expenditure cutbacks "will pose a challenge."

Less gentle was Bruce Little, economics columnist at the *Globe and Mail*. "Sheer gibberish," was how he described Collins' 3.8 percent growth forecast, and the rest of his article on B.C. Liberal fiscal policy used such descriptions as "vapid," "sheer lunacy," "goofiness" and "fantasy."

A month later, fired economist David Bond penned a somber assessment in the *National Post*. The B.C. Liberals' fiscal experiment of "dramatic tax cuts and little else" had "a very high risk of failure," he wrote. As foreseen by the economist in January before he was fired, the province's largest export markets, the United States and Japan, indeed were "experiencing economic downturns."

According to Bond, the Campbell government could minimize long-term damage by taking "a more immediate and aggressive approach to expenditure control." In other words, dramatic tax cuts had to be matched by dramatic reductions in government spending. But Gordon Campbell had promised to maintain health and education funding at current levels, effectively placing "more than 70 percent of the budget beyond reach."

As the summer of 2001 drew to a close, Bond predicted a looming provincial deficit of about $3 billion. But he was wrong; the shortfall would be much larger than that.

Crash of the 'yogic flyer'

B.C.'s first quarterly report for 2001-02 was released on September 13, two days after Islamic terrorists destroyed the World Trade Centre in New York City and attacked the Pentagon building in Washington, D.C. Finance minister Collins made news of his own by finally admitting that deep spending cuts were needed to pay for the summer's enormous tax reductions. As Collins put it, the Campbell government had "some difficult and possibly unpopular decisions to make over the next few months."

Economist David Bond had prophesied way back in January that the international and B.C. economies were slowing noticeably. As a consequence, the quarterly report now showed that British Columbia's annual deficit and the public debt were climbing above the already large estimates offered just six weeks earlier in Collins' mini-budget.

Collins' disconsolate demeanor prompted Vaughn Palmer, the *Vancouver Sun*'s political columnist, to suggest a similarity between the flight instructor-cum-finance minister who thought tax cuts would automatically lift government revenues, and a levitating disciple of the Natural Law Party. "The Liberals' own yogic flyer," Palmer wrote, "has come crashing to earth."

But there was little humour on display when the increasingly glum B.C. Liberal government held an open cabinet meeting on October 3. The week before, Campbell had sent his cabinet ministers a letter ordering them to prepare three budget-cutting scenarios. With the exception of the health and education portfolios, all departments had to envisage funding cuts of 20 percent, 35 percent and 50 percent.

"To get to zero [a balanced budget] by 2004-05," Collins explained to his dispirited colleagues, "we need to bring the rest of government down [from $7.6 billion] to about $4.9 billion, or about a 35 percent reduction on average." Some departments might suffer more, and others less, but all would have to cut staff and programs. "When you start talking about these numbers, it's going to be a smaller government," he said. "That's going to mean fewer people working for government, most likely, in most ministries."

Gone was talk of summertime tax cuts quickly jump-starting the economy. "We're not forecasting big growth in revenues in any way, shape or form" before fiscal year 2004-05, Collins admitted.

Soon thereafter, a TD Economics report showed why Collins was increasingly pessimistic. Under a cheeky headline proclaiming "Deficit as far as the eye can see," the bank study explained that B.C.'s annual shortfalls, without aggressive cutbacks, would quickly balloon to the $3.5 − 4.0 billion level and stay there for the foreseeable future.

It wasn't supposed to go this way. Campbell and Collins had delivered immense tax cuts for their party's high-income and business supporters, ramped-up government expenditures in the belief that tax cuts would pay for themselves, and thought they could quickly grow out of the predictably huge deficits that soon appeared. All but the most fervent supply-siders found that scenario dubious, and now the September 11 attacks had further slowed a sluggish global economy.

"British Columbia is in horrible shape," wrote Bruce Little of the *Globe and Mail*. "Having leaped into a 25 percent personal income tax cut without looking hard enough at its economic prospects, B.C.'s new Liberal government now faces a string of massive deficits, far bigger than any runup by its NDP predecessor."

Premier Campbell appeared unconcerned by such criticism. Speaking to the party faithful at a B.C. Liberal convention in October, he quoted the German poet Goethe: "Whatever you do or dream you can do, begin it," he said. "Boldness has genius, power and magic."

But a few weeks later, on November 20, neither genius nor magic was evident in what the Campbell government called its "comprehensive workforce adjustment strategy." Intended to downsize B.C.'s public service by up to 11,550 positions, the announcement prepared government workers for the firings and layoffs scheduled to occur shortly after the Christmas holidays.

The next day, when Collins issued the government's second quarterly report, it became clear why the B.C. Liberals had become rabid budget-cutters. Revenue estimates were continuing to fall, down now by another $500 million. The weakened revenues indicated that even though much of the forecast allowance was going to be spent, deficits in the consolidated revenue fund and the summary accounts were going to rise even higher than anticipated in the July mini-budget.

There was little hope on the economic horizon. Collins, the rookie finance minister, finally admitted that his projection of 3.8 percent economic growth in 2002 had been too optimistic. His new forecast: a minuscule 0.6 percent.

As 2001 drew to a close, no political observer could call it a year of half measures. The B.C. Liberals had won a massive electoral majority. Weeks later they simultaneously introduced huge tax cuts and enormous spending increases. Those dice had been rolled but the economy came up stalled, and then ministries other than health and education were ordered to slash expenditures by up to 50 percent. Thousands of public employees were expected to lose their jobs.

The quote of the year came from David Bond, the HSBC economist who lost his job after criticizing the B.C. Liberals' fiscal and economic plans. "I could be tempted to say, 'I told you so,' but I shouldn't," said Bond, in response to media enquiries. "After all, Mr. Collins, who was saying there wouldn't be a deficit, is a certified flight instructor and all I've got is a PhD in economics."

Back to taxing

A deficit of more than four billion dollars for 2002-03. That was the crimson red bottom line on the B.C. Liberals' first full-year budget, leaked early to the news media to prepare British Columbians for the shock.

It was a staggering figure. By comparison, the NDP's two "fudge-it" budgets (in 1995-96 and 1996-97), which angered many ordinary British Columbians and outraged the B.C. Liberals and their business supporters, had incurred summary account deficits of $318 million and $385 million. Now the Campbell government intended to incur a shortfall almost six times the combined total of the two fudged NDP budgets — in just a single fiscal year.

Moreover, the New Democrats had recorded a summary accounts surplus of $1.4 billion in their last full fiscal year before being defeated in 2001. How could British Columbia's finances so quickly turn from a large surplus to a gigantic deficit? There were three reasons, although the Campbell government allowed just one: the economic downturn had suppressed provincial revenues. Unmentioned were the other two: their own tax cuts and spending hikes.

On budget day, Collins revealed that the estimated deficit for 2002-03 would be $3.65 billion. To this figure he added another $750 million in forecast allowance, for a nearly-unbelievable total shortfall of $4.4 billion. Yet this was but part of the story: the deficit would have been even higher had Collins not hit unsuspecting British Columbians with a barrage of tax and fee hikes.

Just eight months after bringing in treasury-busting tax cuts, the Campbell government abruptly reversed course and raised taxes and fees by near-record amounts. Surprisingly, the B.C. Liberal tax measures were comparable in total revenue to the increases inflicted on B.C. taxpayers a decade earlier by Mike Harcourt's NDP government.

(In 1992, the New Democrats had boosted taxes by $681.5 million for the then-current fiscal period, and $758.5 million over a full fiscal year. The next year, in 1993, the respective figures were $636.5 million and $803.5 million. Again, the latter budget, which introduced the proposed property surtax, had so infuriated then-Vancouver mayor Gordon Campbell that he had led public protests against the Harcourt government.)

The B.C. Liberals' 2002-03 budget raised Medical Services Plan premiums by 50 percent for an extra $392 million over a full fiscal year. Collins boosted the sales tax to 7.5 percent for an additional $250 million, and jacked up the tobacco tax to get another $150 million per year. These and other measures were expected to enhance government revenues by a whopping $736 million in the current fiscal year, and $778 million in a full-fiscal year. It was a stunning about-face after the previous summer's massive tax cuts.

Collins' fiscal plan also included spending cuts totaling nearly a billion dollars annually. The human resources department planned to reduce its budget by $549 million through a redesigned income assistance program. The Ministry of Children and Family Services sought to cut spending by $146 million by moving at-risk children "from contracted care to foster care" and to save another $90 million by altering the living arrangements for disabled adults. The corrections branch in the Ministry of Public Safety and Solicitor General aimed to reduce spending by $44 million by adopting something called "risk-based supervision" for convicted criminals. And the attorney general's department intended to save $9 million with the closure of 24 courthouses.

These and other cuts were expected to lower yearly spending by a total of $974 million in 2004-05. But most were scheduled to occur toward the end of the three-year period. Until then, huge fiscal deficits would be recorded.

This combination of tax increases and spending reductions allowed Collins to claim that a balanced budget would appear three years hence. At first glance it seemed impossible: the planned shortfall in year one was $4.4 billion; in year two, $1.8 billion; and then in year three (2004-05), a "zero" deficit.

Indeed, closer examination revealed a piece of accounting trickery: Collins had not included a forecast allowance for either of the latter two years. (As explained earlier, the forecast allowance is a line-item budget expense to cover unforeseen rises in expenditure or shortfalls in revenues.)

It was an omission that sharply contrasted with the inflated $1.25-billion forecast allowance the B.C. Liberal-friendly "Financial Review Commission" had injected into projected NDP budgets to manufacture a $5-billion deficit that the Campbell government claimed to have inherited from the NDP. (See sidebar.) A double standard was on display.

B.C.'s business community shared in the hypocrisy. The captains of industry — often vocal in denouncing tax increases and fiscal deficits — might have been expected to recoil in horror at the record-shattering deficit, colossal tax hikes, and dubious balanced-budget plan in the Campbell government's first full-year budget. But such was not the case.

Instead, business representatives warmly embraced the document and its contents. The Vancouver Board of Trade played the role of head cheerleader, issuing a "report card" giving the B.C. Liberals an "A+" for "Economic Vision," an "A" for "Spending Control," and an "Overall" rating of "B+."

"Ridiculous" was how political columnist Vaughn Palmer viewed the report card, which he suggested illustrated "a double standard on debt and deficits." The business response to the 2002-03 budget "tends to reinforce the notion that there are bad deficits and good deficits, bad debt and good debt," Palmer wrote. "The bad are strictly associated with New Democratic Party administrations and the good exclusively the product of the right of centre."

Too true, but looked at another way, the business community's attitude was perfectly understandable. The B.C. Liberals had delivered tax cuts totaling nearly $700 million annually to corporations, and the bulk of the $1.5 billion in yearly personal income tax cuts went to higher-income and wealthy British Columbians. The immediate beneficiaries of these ideological fiscal policies naturally were supportive of their allies in government.

On the other hand, MSP premium and sales tax increases were felt disproportionately by middle- and lower-income residents, as were nearly all of the spending cuts. Over time it became increasingly clear that less-fortunate British Columbians were feeling the pinch of government spending cutbacks. The offices of the mental health advocate, the child, youth and family advocate, and the child commissioner were scrapped. Day care subsidies for lower-income families were reduced, and a before- and after-school program abolished. Elderly British Columbians were hit with a reduction to the seniors' income supplement, and the seniors' subsidized bus pass was eliminated (although later reinstated after a public outcry). The freeze on post-secondary fees was lifted, and tuition fees skyrocketed.

Dozens of services were hit with budget cuts — notably the independent legislative offices which monitored the government, such as the ombudsman and auditor general — and many more wiped out entirely, among them Fisheries BC and the debtor assistance branch.

But there was more to come, notably additional tax hikes. On February 12, 2003, a week before Collins was scheduled to unveil the B.C. Liberals' second full-year budget, Premier Campbell made a televised 'state of the province' address. Fuel taxes, he announced, were being raised by 3.5 cents per litre.

In the budget itself, Collins hiked tax rates on tobacco,

DID LIBERALS 'FIX' B.C.'S ECONOMY?

By WILL McMARTIN

■ Perhaps the single greatest issue which helped propel the B.C. Liberals into government in 2001 was the widespread perception that British Columbia's economy faltered badly during the 1990s, a decade when the New Democratic Party was in power.

Few could argue with the empirical data. The BC Central Credit Union issued an "economic analysis" in November 1999 with the headline, "A

Decade of Decline for B.C." Two months later, the Business Council of BC released a study entitled "British Columbia's Dismal Decade."

Neither report explicitly blamed the New Democrats for the province's falling capital investment, weak GDP (gross domestic product) growth, or declining per capita incomes, but the B.C. Liberals did. "The NDP has taken B.C.'s economy from first to worst in Canada," declared their election platform,

property and insurance premiums. Combined with the higher fuel tax, the total hit to taxpayers was $290 million over a full-fiscal year. So, after cutting tax revenues by $2.1 billion annually in their first two months in office, the Campbell government then raised taxes by nearly $1.1 billion — $778 million in 2002-03, and $290 million in 2003-04 — in their first two budgets. It was a fiscal flip-flop of historic proportions.

The word historic describes another aspect of the Campbell government's 2003-04 budget. For the first time ever, a B.C. budget included federal equalization payments as a line-item source of revenue. Collins had budgeted for an equalization contribution of $675 million in 2003-04, and $700 million in 2004-05, when the budget had to be balanced.

It was increasingly clear that the "zero" deficit promised for the B.C. Liberals' third full-year budget, if it arrived, would be due to tax hikes, spending cuts, and ever-increasing transfers from Ottawa. This was a far cry

---

A New Era for British Columbia.

As a remedy for the province's ailing economy, the B.C. Liberals proposed a "dramatic" reduction in personal income tax rates. This measure, the New Era platform claimed, would stimulate economic growth which in turn would boost government tax revenues. The evidence to date, however, does not bolster their assertion.

Capital investment, for example, has continued to decline. Over the decade following Expo '86, capital investment in B.C. averaged close to 20 percent of GDP. That rate weakened over the 1990s and has continued to fall under the B.C. Liberals: from 2001 to 2003, capital investment averaged 17 percent of GDP.

It is true that the provincial economy in 2004 is stronger than it has been in recent years, but preliminary data shows that GDP growth is about "average" for the past decade and a half. Under the NDP, B.C.'s GDP

from what Campbell, Collins and the New Era election platform had promised voters in 2001, when economic growth stimulated by tax cuts was the means to balancing the government's books.

Before then, however, there was another monster deficit. The operating shortfall for 2003-04 was estimated at $1.8 billion, with a $500-million forecast allowance, making the total budgeted deficit $2.3 billion — the second-biggest in B.C. history, smaller only than the previous year's $4.4-billion shortfall. Once more, business leaders fell over themselves praising the plan, with the president of the Certified General Accountants Association gushing, "These guys are good."

Again it was left to out-of-province commentators to offer a dispassionate analysis. A Scotiabank study noted that "Much of the stimulative effect" of the Campbell government's tax cuts was "still to materialize," while a Royal Bank report described the impact of spending cuts on economic growth as "fiscal drag."

DID LIBERALS 'FIX' ECONOMY? [Cont.]

growth averaged about 3 percent per year. (Source: BC Stats, chained 1997 dollars, revised November 15, 2004.)

The worst performance occurred in 1998 (1.3 percent), and stellar expansion was recorded in 1993 (4.5 percent) and 2000 (4.6 percent.).

Over the first three years of B.C. Liberal government, 2001 to 2003, provincial GDP expanded by 0.9 percent , 3.3 percent and 2.5 percent. The province's second quarterly report for fiscal 2004-05, published in November, put GDP growth forecasts at 3.3 percent for 2004, and 3.6 percent in 2005.

It is evident that B.C.'s economy performed very poorly in 2001, improved somewhat in 2002 and 2003, and in 2004 is slightly above the NDP average. Perhaps an accurate assessment would be that 2004 is an average year in terms of GDP growth over the past decade or so, but appears much better in comparison to the three years which

A sobering assessment was offered by the BMO Financial Group. "Reading the budget speech, one is led to think that British Columbia has reached the promised land, or at least can see it across the river. In reality, British Columbia still faces a couple of years of wandering in the wilderness before its economic and fiscal situation is as rosy as its government portrays."

But Gordon Campbell and Gary Collins did not have a "couple of years"; they had promised to deliver a balanced budget by 2004-05. Could they do it?

The Ottawa windfall

Gary Collins' fourth budget was introduced in the legislature on February 17, 2004. His first, the 2001 minibudget, had a summary accounts deficit of $1.5 billion. His second, in 2002, introduced an enormous shortfall of $4.4 billion, and his third, in 2003, had a $2.3 billion deficit. (The actual year-end deficits were slightly smaller than outlined in Collins' budgets. In 2001-02, the

preceded it. Nonetheless, 2004 does not at this time appear to be close to the exceptional growth rates recorded in 1993 and 2000.

Two events in 2001 had a significant impact on British Columbia; indeed, the entire world. The first was the economic recession in the United States, which prompted that country's Federal Reserve Bank to aggressively cut interest rates to their lowest levels in four decades. The second was the People's Republic of China formally joining the World Trade Organization (WTO).

The first development resulted in a boom in residential construction in the United States and elsewhere around the world as other countries' central banks followed the Americans in slashing interest rates. As a producer and exporter of lumber, plywood and other forest products, B.C. benefited from the hot global housing market. Lumber prices, which

deficit was $2.7 billion, although this properly was reduced to $1.3 billion after adoption of joint-trusteeship for public sector pension plans. The 2002-03 shortfall was $3.3 billion, and the 2003-04 deficit, $1.3 billion.)

Over that period, British Columbia's accumulated deficit soared from $3.5 billion to more than $9.3 billion, while the province's debt climbed from $33.6 billion to $37.3 billion.

The B.C. Liberals seemed unembarrassed by their abysmal fiscal record, holding out hope that a single balanced budget might erase the gallons of red ink spilled in their first three years in office. And so on February 17, 2004, after three massive deficits and billions of dollars in additional debt, Gary Collins unveiled a budget with a small surplus of $100 million. He also made another attempt at cutting taxes, this time by a mere $9 million.

But despite the tiny surplus, British Columbia's debt was expected to climb to nearly $39.5 billion in 2004-05,

DID LIBERALS 'FIX' ECONOMY? [Cont.]

averaged $345 per thousand board feet in 2000, jumped to a peak of $629 in May 2004.

B.C. exports peaked at $33.7 billion in 2000, and then went into a three-year tailspin, dropping to just $28.5 billion in 2003. But a resurgence led by forest products is underway in 2004, and the total value of B.C.'s exports surged past the $3-billion mark in May.

Residential home construction also boomed in British Columbia. After slumping to little

more than 14,000 in 2000, housing starts are expected to surpass 31,000 in 2004. As a result, construction employment has sky-rocketed: where there were fewer than 113,000 persons working in construction in 2000, that figure exceeded 167,000 in October 2004. These construction jobs have more than offset losses in the manufacturing, forestry, mining and fishing sectors.

China's entry into the WTO, and concomitant reduction in

and then higher-still to $40.5 billion in 2005-06. This was because the B.C. Liberals had changed the government's accounting presentation for their third full-year budget.

(The new presentation, called GAAP — generally accepted accounting principles — covers not only the provincial government and Crown corporations, but also schools, universities, colleges and health authorities. Under GAAP, capital expenditures are amortized over the useful life of each asset. So, when Victoria spends a large sum of money for, say, a school or hospital, only a fraction of the total construction cost is recorded in the year it is built; the rest is spread over several decades.)

Not only did this accounting change allow the B.C. Liberals to spend more money than was actually counted in their third full-year budget, it makes it impossible to determine if their original balanced-budget plan worked. An examination of the province's consolidated revenue fund (CRF), however, shows that Campbell and Collins were well wide of the mark, with spending $881 million

tariff barriers to trade, signifies that populous country's formal entry into the global marketplace. Between 1990 and 1999, B.C.'s exports to China grew by 190 percent, but remained relatively small at just $845 million. Pulp represented half of that value, while paper and fish products were eight percent each.

In 2003, for the first time, the value of B.C. exports to China exceeded $1 billion. This is a fraction of exports to the United States ($18.8 billion) and Japan ($3.6 billion), but B.C. manufacturers and the provincial government are working to develop a market for lumber and other wood products.

A more immediate impact on B.C. has been China's voracious demand for commodities, and the subsequent rise in global mineral prices. Copper, for example, averaged $0.71 (Canadian) per pound in 1999 and hit a peak of $1.81 in March 2004. Mineral exploration and pro-

higher than initially forecast, although revenues were also $633 million above target. As a result, instead of having a $197 million CRF surplus (as was promised in the 2002-03 budget), the estimates for 2004-05 showed a deficiency of $51 million.

It is a moot point, however, for windfall monies began flowing into the provincial treasury over the course of the 2004-05 fiscal year. In November, the second quarterly report showed that the annual surplus had exploded from the original $100 million to more than $1.9 billion (and could exceed $2.2 billion). The biggest source of new monies was an unexpected $941 million in B.C.'s equalization entitlement from Ottawa.

British Columbians barely had time to digest their fiscal bonanza when Gary Collins made another surprising announcement: he was quitting politics to become president of a small regional airline.

DID LIBERALS 'FIX' ECONOMY? [Cont.]

duction around the world, and in B.C., has surged as a result.

A 2004 study by the Conference Board of Canada sought to explain B.C.'s improving economy, and offered this: "Heightened construction activity, along with a rebound in manufacturing, mining, and utilities output, will enable the goods-producing industries to churn out solid growth this year and next." In other words, foreign demand for B.C.'s natural resource exports stimulates economic activity in this province. Of course, this has been the case in British Columbia for more than a century, regardless of which party is in government.

Summing up

"First you gather all your facts, then you distort them as you can." Mark Twain's advice has been taken to heart by British Columbia's politicians in recent decades, and the Campbell government is no exception.

The B.C. Liberals claim that their fiscal policies profoundly improved the province's fiscal and economic fortunes. As Gary Collins declared in his 2004 budget speech, the government "laid a firm foundation of good fiscal management; a solid foundation for economic growth; and a firm foundation for sustainable social programs." But there is a striking absence of empirical evidence to support that claim. (See "Did B.C. Liberals 'Fix' the Economy?", p. 158.)

There is no doubt the B.C. Liberals' tax policies shifted the province's overall revenue burden in two ways. First, by lowering "progressive" tax rates (such as personal and corporate income taxes) while increasing "regressive" levies (the sales tax, MSP premiums and post-secondary tuition), the government tilted the emphasis away from businesses, and higher-income and wealthy British Columbians, toward middle- and lower-income individuals. Second, reducing provincial tax revenues and increasing the province's reliance on federal transfers has moved the revenue burden from B.C. taxpayers to Canadians across the country.

The former has been criticized by the Campbell government's political opponents as "unfair," but it remains to be seen — and likely never will be proved — whether it has a beneficial or negative effect on B.C.'s public finances. As for the latter, it hardly seems a positive development that British Columbia is more dependent upon Ottawa for revenue.

To their credit, and as they promised in the 2001 general

Revenue by Source

	NDP Actual 2000-01	B.C. Liberal Forecast 2004-05
Taxation revenue		
Personal income	5,963	5,080
Corporate income	1,054	1,214
Social service	3,625	4,091
Fuel	715	891
Tobacco	460	676
Property	1,452	1,647
Property transfer	262	600
Other	772	540
SUBTOTAL	14,303	14,739
Natural Resources		
Natural gas royalties	1,249	1,419
Columbia River Treaty	632	260
Other energy and minerals	669	597
Forests	1,341	1,405
Water and other resources	308	302
SUBTOTAL	4,199	3,983
Other revenue		
Medical Services Plan premiums	894	1,407
Post secondary fees	440	832
Other healthcare-related fees	411	178
Motor vehicle licences and permits	339	377
Other fees and licences	1,068	838
Investment earnings	1,438	754
Sales of goods and services	966	1,300
SUBTOTAL	4,199	3,983
Contributions from the federal government		
Health and social transfers	2,619	3,402
Equalization	—	980
Other federal contributions	665	733
SUBTOTAL	3,284	5,115

(Continued on next page)

NDP VS. B.C. LIBERALS

	NDP Actual 2000-01	B.C. Liberal Forecast 2004-05
Commercial Crown corporation net income		
BC Hydro	549	210
Liquor Distribution Branch	642	760
BC Lotteries	562	842
BC Rail	(7)	236
ICBC	139	355
Other	4	6
Accounting adjustments	(164)	—
SUBTOTAL	3,284	5,115
TOTAL REVENUE	**29,983**	**32,619**
Expense by Function		
Health	9,555	11,776
Social Services	3,276	2,669
Education	7,856	8,952
Protection of persons and property	1,313	1,212
Transportation	1,577	1,408
Natural resources and economic development	1,776	1,377
Other	590	858
Contingencies	—	240
General government	435	463
Debt servicing	2,050	1,420
TOTAL EXPENSE	**28,428**	**30,375**
TOTAL REVENUE	**29,983**	**32,619**
TOTAL EXPENSE	**28,428**	**30,375**
Surplus	1,555	2,244
(*Forecast allowance*)		(300)
	1,555	1,944

(*SOURCE: All numbers have been converted to GAAP — generally accepted accounting principles — by the finance ministry. The revenues and expenditures for fiscal year 2000-01 are from the "Budget and Fiscal Plan, 2004-05 to 2006-07," pp. 144 and 145, and for fiscal 2004-05 from the "Second Quarterly Report on the Economy, Fiscal Situation and Outlook, Fiscal Year 2004-05," pp. 36 and 41.)*

election, the B.C. Liberals did balance the province's books in the final year of their four-year mandate. And, in fact, the second quarterly report for 2004-05 indicates that a record surplus will appear when the public accounts are published in the summer of 2005, some time after the general election scheduled for May 17.

The NDP also had a record surplus before suffering an electoral defeat of historic proportions in 2001. Indeed, one might conclude that the Campbell government's first term in office will end as it began: with an overflowing treasury. Unmentioned by the B.C. Liberals will be the intervening period, the four turbulent years marked by "dramatic" tax cuts and spending hikes, and the abrupt about-face with massive tax increases and spending reductions.

Debated by many will be the question of how great was the change wrought to British Columbia's public sector by the Campbell government. The best measurement is to compare the province's finances in the NDP's last full year in government (re-stated for GAAP) to the B.C. Liberals' most recent full fiscal year (as outlined in the 2004-05 second quarterly report).

Contrary to popular belief, the Campbell government did not reduce overall government expenditures. Total spending under the NDP was $28.4 billion; under the B.C. Liberals, $30.4 billion. Health expenditures increased by $2.2 billion to $11.8 billion, while education spending (which includes both K-12 and post-secondary) rose by more than $1 billion to nearly $9 billion. Together, health and education expenditures as a proportion of total government spending climbed from 61 percent to 68 percent.

In a replay of his tenure at Vancouver city hall and the Greater Vancouver Regional District, Gordon Campbell also allowed the province's administrative costs to rise.

"General government" expenditures moved upward from $435 million to $463 million.

Significant declines were recorded in two categories of expenditure. Social services had the biggest reduction, with spending falling by $600 million to $2.7 billion. Debt servicing charges reflected the global decline in interest rates, falling from $2.1 billion to just $1.4 billion, even as the government's total debt climbed ever higher. Other categories of expenditure recorded slight decreases.

On the revenue side, it is painfully evident that the Campbell government's tax cuts failed to pay for themselves. The government's total income rose from $30 billion under the NDP, to $32.6 billion under the B.C. Liberals, but nearly all of the increase was due to higher transfer payments from Ottawa.

Total taxation revenue was nearly static, rising by $436 million to $14.7 billion. That represents an increase of just 3 percent over four years, well short of that required to cover population growth and inflation. After several years in decline, receipts from corporation income tax rose slightly to $1.2 billion in 2004-05. Personal income tax revenue is just $5 billion, 15 percent lower than before the Campbell cuts.

The sharpest increase in tax receipts was from the property transfer tax, up 129 percent to $600 million on a strong residential real estate market. Revenues from retail sales, fuel, tobacco and property rose slightly.

The largest real revenue growth occurred in federal transfers. The New Democrats received $3.3 billion from Ottawa in 2000-01; the B.C. Liberals estimate the comparable figure will be $5.1 billion in 2004-05, an increase of 67 percent.

Net income for the province's commercial Crown corporations climbed from $1.7 billion to $2.4 billion. The biggest gain was at B.C. Lotteries Corp, up $280 million to $842 million (a 50 percent increase which reflects the B.C. Liberals' expansion of gambling activities).

Dramatic revenue increases were recorded from two other sources. Medical Service Plan premiums soared by 47 percent to $1.4 billion, and post-secondary tuition fees sky-rocketed 89 percent to $832 million. It is evident that much of the increased education expenditure was financed by students.

The bottom line is that the New Democrats had a surplus of nearly $1.6 billion in their final year in government; the B.C. Liberals should record a surplus of about $2.0 billion in their final year. However, both the NDP and B.C. Liberals endured years of deficits before achieving those positive results. It also must be said that the respective windfall surpluses were largely unplanned, and certainly of a magnitude not foreseen by either government.

Of greater concern is the question of whether the most recent surplus marks a fundamental alteration in B.C.'s fiscal situation. For more than two decades British Columbia has endured sporadic economic growth and weak provincial finances; have we really turned the corner?

After coming to power in 2001, Gordon Campbell and his party inherited a massive surplus and then over a three year period created a sea of red ink by cutting taxes and raising expenditures in the face of economic recession. They then desperately attempted to reverse course through tax hikes and spending cuts, and finally, on the eve of a general election with a huge boost in federal government transfers, finally produced a balanced budget.

There are only two certainties here. First, it likely will be many years hence before any B.C. politician promises voters that tax cuts will pay for themselves. And second, aspiring novelists and B.C. politicians will probably continue to follow the advice that Mark Twain offered more than a century ago; they will gather the facts, and then distort them as they can.

CHAPTER 7

High Rollers

By DAVID BEERS AND
BARBARA MᶜLINTOCK

'WE HAVE to find ways of having a respectful and open public debate about what we're trying to accomplish. When you look at the issues, I don't know anyone who doesn't want a great public health care system and a great public education system. So we have to change the way we have conversations about that." This was Gordon Campbell in the February 2005 issue of *BC Business* magazine going for, it seemed, the role of premier as visionary conciliator. "Our big challenge as we go through the next 20 years is to find new ways to include people."

Perhaps Campbell was hoping to salve some bruises among the B.C. electorate. But many of those bruises remain deep because the game has been so rough over the past four years. Very often the governing strategy of the Campbell Liberals has seemed to be less about including new people, more about rewarding their most loyal existing base: namely business people, social conservatives, and Lower Mainland males. Three particularly divisive moments come to mind.

The first was the referendum on aboriginal treaty making. Given the magnitude of his win, Campbell could have backed off his campaign promise to hold one. But he pressed forward with apparent relish. This despite strong opposition from not only natives, but the federal government, labour groups, environmental organizations, the Anglican Church, Jewish and Muslim groups, and women's groups. Some believed the ballot overstepped the Charter of Rights and Freedoms. Others saw pro-government bias in the wording of the questions. Veteran pollster Angus Reid called the referendum "amateurish" and "one-sided."

Another fierce critic was the noted historian Michael Ignatieff, who does in fact spend a lot of time thinking about new ways to include people. Ignatieff has written that as Canada works through Quebec nationalism, aboriginal claims and similar issues, it offers the world a nuanced model for balancing individual and group rights. But in B.C. Ignatieff saw the opposite, something more akin to America's southern white majority voting on whether to discriminate against blacks. The First Nations in B.C have a legitimate claim to land and the preservation of their language and culture, so it's a bad idea to let their fate be decided by the general population at the ballot box, argued Ignatieff. "I think referenda can institutionalize majority tyranny."

None of this moved Campbell. "I don't understand why a referendum for the general public, including aboriginal people, is wrong," he said. "People will get a chance to vote."

In the end, about one out of three B.C. voters did mail in their ballots. Who won depended on which side you were on. The government boasted that 80 percent of those who voted sided with the government's principles, which included denying First Nations tax exemptions, autonomous rule, and land expropriated from public parks or private hands. That left the two thirds who did not vote. In defiance, some of them burned their ballots, others scissored theirs into snowflakes. The dissenters would say that 75 percent of B.C. voters either boycotted or voted no on the referendum. And that it didn't matter anyway. "You cannot take away our rights by referendum, just simply because you are the majority and you can outvote us," said Herb George, spokesman for the First Nations Summit, the day the results were announced, July 4, 2002. The *Globe and Mail* headline that day: "B.C. and Natives Square Off."

In the spring of 2004 it was time for members of B.C.'s Hospital Employees' Union to run up against the limits of the Campbell government's inclusiveness. Some 43,000 health workers had hit the picket lines. They'd done so after seeing 8,500 fellow workers lose their jobs to low-paying private firms. Their employers hadn't budged on a 15 percent pay cut, longer work weeks, and contracting out thousands more jobs. Four days after the HEU workers walked out, surgeries were getting cancelled and public sentiment sat on a knife's edge. The government's response was to hastily pass Bill 37, which imposed everything the employers wanted and even more: a clawback. Give back 15 percent of your pay going back weeks before the strike, workers were told. Many of those workers were women, people of colour, people who gathered up and washed soiled sheets and dirty bed pans. Never mind that the hospital workers were now under court order to return to their jobs. Bill 37 was the catalyst for a wave of solidarity strikes by other unions that threatened to become a general strike before a truce finally was brokered, late in the night of May 2, by the HEU, the BC Federation of Labour, and the Campbell government.

As in the case of the treaty referendum, there was a way to argue that Gordon Campbell had come out the winner. His side had given up its aim of shifting 6,000 hospital jobs from public to private contracts, but 600 were still slated for outsourcing as, to his business base, the premier had shown himself a tough foe of unions. Had the strike, however, really needed to escalate to the point of nearly shutting down the province? And was Bill 37 just too harsh?

It is a given in political science in B.C. — and in most other places as well — that governments virtually always win public sector strikes, especially once the courts have ruled those strikes to be illegal. But a McIntyre and Mustel poll conducted for Global TV showed clearly that Gordon Campbell had managed to lose it. When push came to shove, just 51 percent of those surveyed said they disapproved of the HEU's strategy and tactics, compared to 65 percent who disapproved of how Campbell and his cabinet had acted. Asked about how they viewed Campbell's personal performance, a full 47 percent said it had made them think worse of him as premier. Only six percent said it had improved their view of him.

Apparently, a large majority of British Columbians weren't impressed by the oversimplified union-bashing spin that Campbell was attempting to put on the issue. They realized that it was a much more complex event than the government was making it out to be. Even after the poll was released, Campbell and his ministers continued to put 100 percent of the blame on the HEU for everything that happened.

The third and perhaps most telling tale in this trilogy is Gordon Campbell's handpicking of the candidate to run in the high stakes Surrey-Panorama Ridge byelection in October 2004. Campbell anointed Mary Polak, a white, socially conservative Surrey school board chair who had failed in her legal crusade to ban school books depicting same-sex parents. That gave her a high profile, though not necessarily for finding "new ways to include people." And she took a drubbing on polling day, finishing 20 points behind the NDP candidate, Jagrup Brar, who, as it happened, benefited from a sense among Indo-Canadians that they were not sufficiently included in the thoughts and actions of the B.C. Liberal government's leadership.

There was no way to spin this one as a Campbell victory; in fact, as former Socred advisor Will McMartin observed in the Tyee, the loss "was one of the worst midterm performances in recent memory by a governing party in a government-held riding ... Nearly six of every 10 former B.C. Liberal backers abandoned the party either by not voting, or voting for a different party." This despite the Liberals vastly outspending the NDP on the election, and Gordon Campbell himself feverishly working the phones to up voter turnout.

Which made it odd to some observers that Mary Polak was promised another go at it for the B.C. Liberals, this time in a Langley riding, in the May election. That added fuel to speculation that Gordon Campbell's party, rather than blurring its ideological borders ever more widely and inclusively, actually was lurching farther and harder right.

WHO'S GREENER: GORDON OR THE GOVERNATOR?

By MARCIE GOOD

■ Who says a pro-business government can't be cutting-edge green? Cast an eye south, to Arnold Schwarzenegger's California. There exists a bold agenda to improve air, water and quality of life to keep the Golden State's work force vital in a competitive global economy.

Schwarzenegger's campaign didn't inspire high hopes on the environmental front. Consider his own vehicle, the gas-guzzling Hummer which seemed to confirm his persona as the Governator, running over anything in his way. But soon after his October election victory, Arnold confounded his critics by his choice of Terry Tamminen as secretary of the Environmental Protection Agency. Most recently, Tamminen was executive director of Environment Now, a foundation aimed at protecting California's environment and natural resources. And once in office, Schwarzenegger's team produced a position paper laying

MLA Lynn Stephens, more centrist than Polak, stated publicly that she didn't think Polak should try to take over the Langley riding even though Stephens had already announced she wouldn't be running again herself. Polak's views, she said, did not fit with the views of a majority of Langley residents. The rising powers within the party, however, tended to be those with more socially conservative views, such as Solicitor General Rich Coleman and Transportation Minister Kevin Falcon.

Further evidence of the government's rightward shift went into the mail in January 2005: "The Honourable Gordon Campbell, Premier of British Columbia, requests the pleasure of your company at a reception in honour of the National Caucus of the Conservative Party of Canada at the Royal British Columbia Museum? Please present this invitation at the reception registration table. Dress: business attire." Campbell's Liberals would end up throwing a bash for Stephen Harper precisely at the moment when the Conservative leader was muttering

out ambitious commitments to clean air and water. Promises:

● cut air pollution statewide by up to 50 percent;

● protect California's coastline and waterways, including a permanent ban on offshore drilling;

● solve the state's electrical energy crisis, with a goal to derive 33 percent of its power from renewable sources by 2020;

● protect and restore California's parks, specifically mentioning the Sierra Nevada which had been eyed by the Bush adminis-

tration for an expansion of logging; and

● restore cities, including improvements to mass transit; and enforce laws protecting the environment. Schwarzenegger even promised to convert one of his Hummers to run on hydrogen.

Charged with jump-starting California's sluggish business climate, Schwarzenegger kept insisting: "Jobs versus the environment is a false choice." In fact, his ambitious "Action Plan

about forcing an election over same-sex marriage, which happened to be Mary Polak's favourite bugaboo.

Meanwhile the list of names of recent departures from the party seemed for the most part to be cut from significantly different cloth. Topping the list: Former Deputy Minister Christy Clark and former Finance Minister Gary Collins. These were, arguably, the two strongest and most powerful voices in cabinet for genuine Liberal thinking — a philosophy of financial caution and accountability but a small-l liberal stand on social issues such as gay rights and even abortion.

But then, Clark and Collins were also two politicians with the misfortune to be tied, however tangentially, to a bulging file aptly labeled by the RCMP. Investigators called it Operation Everywhichway.

Scandal, Everywhichway

British Columbia, has never been a province where policy plays a leading role in deciding the outcome of elec-

WHO'S GREENER? [Cont.]

for California's Environment" states that clean air and water would make for a more productive workforce and a healthier economy.

In B.C., the government has followed a sharply divergent path. While Gov. Schwarzenegger appointed a well-known environmentalist as his guardian of the trees, water and earth, back in 2001 Premier Campbell terminated the watchdog office of Commissioner for Environment and Sustainability before

the post could be filled.

Gov. Schwarzenegger has publicly promised several times that he will fight expected challenges to cleaner air laws. Campbell's Liberals, however, have weakened a network of environmental protection laws put in place over a series of decades.

In his February 2004 Throne Speech, Premier Campbell promised that half of new electricity produced by BC Hydro would come from clean, renewable sources. The year before, Camp-

tions. Rather, for at least the past half-century, the politics of the province have been defined by scandal. From the adventures of Flying Phil Gaglardi to Bill Vander Zalm's Fantasy Gardens, from Dave Stupich's fraudulent use of bingo funds to Glen Clark's controversial rear deck, British Columbians have learned not to be surprised when they hear that their politicians are in conflicts of interest, are under investigation by the RCMP, or are even charged criminally.

Indeed, the cynicism spreads so deep that many citizens were waiting after the election of the Campbell government for the first major scandal to break. Not because they necessarily thought that the Campbell Liberals were any worse than any other party, but simply because they had come to believe that scandals were a matter of course in B.C. politics, no matter what party was in government. Many were actually surprised when for more than two years after the election, the Campbell administration seemed untouched by scandal. (There was, of course,

bell pledged "an environmental framework that sets an example not just for our country but for the world," adding that "environmental sustainability and public policy is a critical part of our social and economic future in British Columbia."

But around the same time, a coalition of environmental groups in B.C. gave the Liberal government a failing grade for its "environmental stewardship."

Within B.C.'s own Ministry of Water, Land and Air Protection, most workers see standards eroding, according to a newly revealed internal review. Only 27 percent of employees surveyed said they believe that their ministry uses good science to support policy decisions, according to George Heyman, president of the BC Government and Service Employees' Union, which obtained and made public the review ordered by the B.C. government. Seventy percent of Environmental Protection branch workers think their

Campbell's incident of drunk driving while on Maui, but observers saw that as a personal foible, not a political scandal).

But when the scandal did break it was, in some ways, on a scale so grandiose as to be previously unknown, even in British Columbia. On December 28, 2003, just three days after Christmas, thousands watched on their television sets as dozens of police officers carried out dozens of boxes of files from the Legislative Buildings themselves. They had been executing a search warrant granted to them by B.C.'s deputy chief Supreme Court judge, the Honorable Patrick Dohm — a search warrant that gave the officers specific permission to enter cabinet ministers' suites of offices to look for evidence. That had not happened before in recent B.C. history. Although political figures had been targeted in investigations, the Legislative Buildings themselves had previously been seen as sacrosanct, a place well separated from the hurly-burly of money-grubbing activities, be they legal or not.

WHO'S GREENER? [Cont.]

department has poor capacity to deal with environmental crises.

In October 2003, the B.C. government designated about 45 million hectares of public land as "working forest," removing most barriers to privatization of B.C.'s public forest lands. Whereas B.C. once had Canada's strongest Environmental Assessment Act, says environmental lawyer David Boyd, we now have its weakest.

Just days into his term, Gov. Schwarzenegger stood up against a Senate move that would have curbed California's right to regulate emissions, in this case from lawnmowers and other small engines. Thanks in part to his lobbying efforts, the measure was quashed.

"It was the kind of thing that very few governors would do," explains Hal Harvey, who worked on Schwarzenegger's transition team as a consultant on greenhouse gases and energy issues. "When Schwarzenegger calls up a Republican Senator,

It soon became clear that the main targets of the police probe — conducted jointly by the Victoria police department and the RCMP — were not themselves elected officials. Rather, they were two ministerial aides — David Basi and Bobby Virk. Basi was arguably the most high-profile ministerial aide in government. He was the senior assistant to Finance Minister Gary Collins, and Collins was rarely seen in the legislative hallways without Basi by his side. One of his main jobs was to assist Collins in his role as House Leader, and he was well-known for taking favoured journalists aside to pass on "tips" and the government's interpretation of political events as they unfolded. Basi, who lived in the Greater Victoria area, was also well known in both provincial and federal riding association circles for orchestrating takeovers of nomination meetings and whole riding associations. From his days at the University of Victoria, he'd been known as the leader of an informal group of young turks nicknamed "Basi's Boys" who would sign up Liberal

they have to listen to him. So having him stand up for environmental issues certainly changes the dynamic altogether."

Another one of Schwarzenegger's pet policies is renewable energy. His administration, he promises, will direct the California Energy Commission to define incentives and implement strategies to meet the 20-percent mark by 2010.

That's a marked contrast to British Columbia, where the government cleared the way for

coal-burning power plants. Two generating plants are currently in the works, one in Campbell River and one in Elk Valley. The B.C. government set new guidelines to regulate certain emissions, but did not address mercury or greenhouse gases. The technology to remove mercury from coal-burning emissions is not yet available.

Perhaps the most striking example of how B.C.'s priorities differ from those of the Golden State is offshore oil exploration.

members by the hundred or arrive en masse at controversial nomination meetings.

Virk, by contrast, was much less well known. He had
been the ministerial aide to Transportation Minister
Judith Reid, and although TV stations had shots of him
walking alongside his minister, he was generally seen as
one of the quiet army of politically-appointed minions
who do their job behind the scenes, drawing very little
attention to themselves personally.

The government also apparently understood the difference in the two men's roles in the power structure. Less
than 24 hours after the search warrants had been executed, Basi was fired outright by the cabinet. Virk, by
contrast, was placed on a paid suspension — a state of
affairs that lasted for more than a year, while he collected
his regular salary without ever setting foot in the Legislative Buildings. Neither Collins nor Campbell ever
gave a cogent explanation of why the two had been
treated so differently. They tried to argue that Basi's role

WHO'S GREENER? [Cont.]

B.C.'s Liberals have pushed the
federal government to lift the
moratorium which has stood
since the early 1970s.

In California, however, this
issue is such a hot button that
Schwarzenegger wants to end it
for good. His environment plan
says he will fight for a permanent ban on all oil drilling in
coastal waters, and that he will
pressure the Bush administration to buy up remaining offshore oil leases. There is a precedent for such a move: the

president made a similar deal to
buy leases off the coast of Florida, where his brother Jeb is governor. Californians have made it
clear that they want to keep their
beaches pristine, without the
threat of a disaster similar to the
oil-well blowout that happened
in 1969 off the coast of Santa Barbara.

*Taken from an article published
April 22, 2004 in the Tyee.*

as assistant to the House Leader made it impossible for him to function while the probe was underway. That, however, never explained why Virk continued to draw a salary while he too was completely non-functioning as far as his role with government went. Speculation continued unabated that Collins or Campbell or someone in cabinet was aware that the charges facing the two might be quite different — but no firm evidence ever emerged to support this theory.

As is inevitable in such cases, the police, and the special prosecutor when appointed, were reluctant to provide many details of just what they were looking for, and judges agreed the details should remain sealed for several months. But what did become clear quite quickly was that the police had not code-named the investigation Operation Everywhichway for nothing. There were allegations that drug-dealing and money-laundering might somehow be involved. Among those under investigation alongside Basi and Virk was a Victoria city police officer, Const. Rob Dosanjh, who was suspended because he had apparently somehow taken advantage of his position on the force to help someone out.

There were suggestions that the investigation was showing links between some of the players involved (and perhaps their money) and the federal Liberal party in B.C. That proved a bitter pill to swallow for cabinet minister Christy Clark. Her husband, Mark Marissen, was head of federal Liberal efforts in the province now that Paul Martin had come to power in Ottawa. Also involved was Christy's brother, Bruce, a former pro-tobacco advocate who had become a major fund-raiser for the federal Liberals in B.C. A search warrant was carried out on Bruce Clark's office, and Marissen opened up some of his files to the Mounties voluntarily, but was never formally faced with a search warrant.

But worst of all for the Campbell administration was the thought that somehow, at the centre of whatever corruption might or might not exist, was the deal to privatize BC Rail. The policy of selling the operating rights to the railway was controversial enough in itself without having scandal attach to it. It was widely seen as breaking an election promise *not* to sell off the railway, no matter how many times Campbell argued that the railway itself wasn't being sold since the province would still own the tracks and railbed. There was much argument that the railway was now actually performing well on the economic side, and could not be considered a deep hole of debt and deficit as the government has argued. There was great concern in northern B.C. that the privatization deal was going to mean the loss of several hundred jobs, almost all of them in Prince George and environs.

The government did not, on top of all that, need allegations that the deal was somehow not on the up-and-up. Oddly, however, the bidder for the railway whose name came up most often in conversation about the scandal was not the winning bidder, CP Rail. It was, in fact, one of the losing proponents, a U.S. firm known as Omnitrax. Just how Omnitrax fit into the scandal when it failed to win the bid has yet to be made clear, but the formal charges laid almost one year to the day from the initial raid showed that its involvement in the bidding process was indeed related to some of the charges now laid.

From the day of the raids, the Campbell government tried to minimize their seriousness and to distance Basi and Virk from the main powerbrokers around the cabinet table. Basi and Virk were described as "government workers" as if they cleaned the toilets or perhaps answered the phones, rather than being accepted as two of the men who were closer to the seat of power than nearly anyone in the Legislative Buildings. Gary Collins said he was surprised Basi's office was large enough to hold all the files the police had removed from it. And cabinet minister after cabinet minister insisted that the BC Rail deal itself was clean. (Though how they could know without talking out of turn to law enforcement personnel remains unknown.)

The investigation lasted almost exactly a year before any action was taken, at least on the political side. Then, less than a week before Christmas 2004, special prosecutor Terrence Robertson announced that specific counts relating to bribery, fraud and corruption would be laid against three men — Basi, Virk and more surprising, Dave Basi's cousin, Aneal, whose name had never before come publicly to the fore in regard to the raid. Aneal had been working in what sounds like a fairly low-level job in the government's Public Affairs Bureau. His previous experience was mainly as an outstanding field hockey player at the University of Victoria. Nonetheless, this too was an order-in-council appointment, meaning the job went to someone recommended through political channels and not necessarily to the best candidate — although some of the bureau staff had long since proved highly competent no matter how they were appointed. Even more interesting were the specific charges against Aneal Basi: he was charged with two counts of money laundering, the money being that which Dave Basi was alleged to have acquired by questionable means. This was the first time that anyone outside the actual investigation had heard of any money actually changing hands. In any case, the Liberal government hastily fired both Virk and Aneal Basi as soon as the charges were announced.

Collins, however, was not there to comment. Just one week earlier he had, in a surprise move, resigned from both cabinet and caucus to run a privately owned airline based out of Vancouver. He insisted there was no link whatsoever between his departure and the charges being announced. Once again, there is not a piece of evidence to contradict him except British Columbians' natural cynicism that the timing was just too, too coincidental.

Neither was Christy Clark in the cabinet by the time the charges were announced. She too resigned, rather publicly and dramatically, talking of wanting to spend more time with her family — and also denying any connection with Operation Everywhichway altogether.

In the hole?

The chance of further fallout from Operation Everywhichway before May 17 remains the wild card of the provincial election. The B.C. Liberals would rather the focus be on their claim to have put the province on firm economic footing. Taxpayer-supported ads singing the economy's praises had ended in mid-January, but by then a powerful group called the Coalition of BC Businesses was well on its way to organizing another messaging blitz along the same lines. A January 27 e-mail to dozens of municipal chambers of commerce around the province from John Winter, President of the BC Chamber of Commerce, laid out the strategy for the Coalition (which, as he explained, "has successful [sic] shielded organizations like ours who shy away from entering the political arena.")

"The Coalition will be undertaking a public communications program which will be rolled out as a lead-up to the provincial election campaign. All members of the Coalition, including the BC Chamber have enthusiastically endorsed the communications proposal and have been active doing fundraising within the business community to pay the freight. Radio and print ads in a wide range of markets are planned for the month of March. We have found that many businesses support the government policy regarding labour and employment and are willing to contribute to the Coalition's efforts as a consequence. If you have members who you think might be interested, we would love to hear about them.

"As we begin to execute the communication strategy, we are looking for your help. We are looking for small business people anywhere in the province who are willing to speak publicly about how the policies of the government have made a difference to their business in the past years, — i.e., 'I've been able to hire 4 more people', 'I have begun to expand my location', or comments of a similar nature. The testimonials would be used in the media campaign.

"Please take a moment to think through your membership lists and contact networks. If you know of someone who may be a suitable candidate, please forward their name and contact information on to the Coalition Coordinator . . ."

And so business was rallying its troops at a moment when the B.C. Liberals were polling even with the resurgent New Democrats, who were themselves tapping networks of labour, community activists, environmentalists, poverty rights workers and women's groups. Four years after the Liberals had won their stunning mandate, the province was as polarized as ever, and though Gordon Campbell was saying in *BC Business* magazine that "We have to find ways of having a respectful and open public debate" and "change the way we have conversations" and "find new ways to include people," a simplistic war of words was shaping up to sound mighty familiar to B.C. voters. Addressing his party's convention a few months earlier, Campbell had named the province's "three major political parties" the Liberals, the Greens and "The BC Federation of Labour."

B.C. Liberal strategists openly declared their intent to relentlessly attack the NDP as a pawn of big labour, and columnists in CanWest newspapers wondered aloud why the NDP couldn't just cut its formal ties to unions. Less discussed was the idea that the B.C. Liberals, who get most of their funding from corporations, should speak uncomfortable truths to business about what it might really take to move B.C. to a long-term sustainable economy. That was a conversation long overdue in B.C.'s political culture, the need for it growing more pressing with every new bulletin about how global warming was melting the ski runs at Whistler, or pine beetles were munching away interior forests.

Instead, voters could be forgiven for shielding their eyes from the bright Las Vegas neon that seemed to blink whenever their politicians began to paint visions of the province's future. They had been asked to take it on faith, after all, that the billion-dollar Olympics gamble would yield a jackpot five years out. That spending $500 million in new ferry construction in Germany rather than here would pay off big. That the condo market in Vancouver was on an unstoppable roll. That the global roulette wheels of foreign currency and commodity prices would be kind to B.C. That tax cuts would work a special mojo, eventually not subtracting but actually adding coin to the government purse.

The people had been told that gambling itself, despite Gordon Campbell's campaign promise to stop its expansion, was going to be allowed to grow and that (addiction and organized crime concerns aside) it would pay off handsomely for British Columbians. And therein lay a metaphor for what Gordon Campbell and his party had done with that mandate handed them four years before. Rather than cautiously keep and expand upon the coalition of voters they had attracted to their cause, they had rolled the dice on controversial neoconservative economic theories and confrontational politics. Those dice had ricocheted around a diverse province, and when they had come to rest, they added up to something considerably less than many of their voters had hoped or expected.

David Beers is founding editor of the Tyee, an online source of news and views for British Columbia (www.thetyee.ca). He has served as senior editor at *Mother Jones*, chief features editor at the *Vancouver Sun*, and has been published in the *Globe and Mail*, the *New York Times*, *Harper's* and many other publications.

Russ Francis is an award-winning legislature reporter and columnist, with a special interest in open government. Francis is an acknowledged expert in the use of B.C.'s freedom of information law. His work has appeared in The Tyee, the *National Post*, *The Province*, *Monday Magazine*, *BC Business*, *New Scientist* and numerous other publications.

Barbara McLintock is a contributing editor for the Tyee. She is the former Victoria bureau chief for the *Province*, a consultant, and the author of two books, *Anorexia's Fallen Angel* and *Smoke Free: How One City Successfully Banned Smoking in All Indoor Public Places*.

Will McMartin is a regular columnist for the Tyee and a regular on CBC Radio's Early Edition. He is a former advisor to the Social Credit Party, a veteran political consultant, and has published the newsletter *BC Politics and Policy*.

Alisa Smith, a regular contributor to the Tyee and a contributing editor for *Vancouver Magazine*, has written for numerous publications including the *Globe and Mail*, *National Post*, *Ottawa Citizen*, *Vancouver Sun*, *Canadian Geographic* and *Outside*.

Chris Tenove is a contributing editor to the Tyee. His reporting for the Tyee on conditions in rural B.C. was nominated for a Webster Award. He has contributed to the *National Post*, CBC Radio, the *Globe and Mail*, *Maclean's*, and *Adbusters*.